D1379775

A Comparative Study of
the Political Communication Styles
of Bill Clinton and Tony Blair

A COMPARATIVE STUDY OF
THE POLITICAL COMMUNICATION STYLES
OF BILL CLINTON AND TONY BLAIR

Olugbenga Chris Ayeni

Studies in Political Science
Volume 31

The Edwin Mellen Press
Lewiston•Queenston•Lampeter

Library of Congress Cataloging-in-Publication Data

Ayeni, Olugbenga Chris.
  A comparative study of the political communication styles of Bill Clinton and Tony Blair
/ Olugbenga Chris Ayeni.
       p. cm. -- (Studies in political science ; v. 31)
  Includes bibliographical references and index.
  ISBN 0-7734-5976-6
  1. Communication in politics--United States--Case Studies. 2. Communication in
politics--Great Britain--Case studies. 3. Presidents--United States--Case studies. 4.
Clinton, Bill, 1946- 5. Prime ministers--Great Britain--Case studies. 6. Blair, Tony, 1953-
I. Title. II. Studies in political science (Lewiston, N.Y.) ; v. 31.

JA85.2.U6A94 2005
324.7--dc22

                                                                    2005054374

This is volume 31 in the continuing series
Studies in Political Science
Volume 31 ISBN 0-7734-5976-6
SPSc Series ISBN 0-7734-7434-X

A CIP catalog record for this book is available from the British Library.

The Edwin Mellen Press
Box 450
Lewiston, New York
USA 14092-0450

The Edwin Mellen Press
Box 67
Queenston, Ontario
CANADA L0S 1L0

The Edwin Mellen Press, Ltd.
Lampeter, Ceredigion, Wales
UNITED KINGDOM SA48 8LT

Printed in the United States of America

This book is dedicated to the loving memory of my mother, Dorcas Folake Ayeni, for her love and affection. We all miss your warm presence in our lives.

Table of Contents

Foreword

Two baby boomer politicians in the United States of America and Great Britain running for the top jobs in their respective countries during the post cold war, post-ideological era seemed to be united not only in a generational bond but from the standpoint of educational attainments, religious practices, choice of wives and professions, youthful vigor, oratorical flourish, campaign acumen and political platforms of striking commonality.

It is natural that both the election campaigns of Bill Clinton in 1996 and Tony Blair in 1997, only a few months apart, held a tremendous fascination for the global press and public in which two politicians with uncommon deftness positioned their parties and their philosophy of governance in a centrist/right direction, marking a departure from the traditional politics of the Democratic Party in the United States and the Labor in Great Britain.

In an important contribution to the discipline of cross-cultural political advertising and communication, Olubenga Christopher Ayeni has analyzed televised advertising messages combined with tapes of party conferences and national conventional speeches of the two candidates employing a variety of qualitative, cultural and critical methods of analysis. The goal is to answer the broad question: how do the patterns of televised messages reflect the political ideologies of the two candidates and their parties and what kinds of verbal, visual and acoustic codes do they use to appeal to the voting publics in their respective countries?

As part of the verbal codes the campaigns used attitudinal language expressing positive judgments for Bill Clinton and Tony Blair, the protagonists and negative judgments on their political opponents. A valuative language containing moral, religious, social, and an aesthetic sense of their people was employed to appeal to the public. Values of compassion, care for the underprivileged, respect for the elderly, love of family, respect for the rule of law, responsibility for self and duty to society were embedded in the messages of Bill Clinton's campaign.

By using a very similar valuative and metaphorical language, Blair emphasized his commitment to the needs of the elderly, right of the children to a high-quality education, lower taxes for the middle-class Britons, clean and safe environment, and a dramatic improvement of the health care delivery system. Both leaders wished to project a forward looking, optimistic vision for their country, and, therefore, Bill Clinton used the metaphor of constructing a bridge to the 21st century by providing a more efficient, and caring but a smaller government, while Blair offered a new, vibrant leadership, a Labor party with new ideological postures with pragmatic underpinnings.

Many studies of political message systems in the United States offer quantitative examination of the incidence of themes, and other basic features of campaigns, but Ayeni in this study goes off the beaten track and uses a multiplicity of analytical methods combining features of ideological, narrative and semiological/stucturalist modes of examining texts. This kind of triangulation of qualitative methods allows the author to go underneath the manifest content of the text and bring out the deeply embedded meanings of speech acts, uses of metaphors and metonyms, on the one hand, and the various use of visual and other symbolic and iconic signs on the other. By attempting this comparative study of campaign cultures in two major English-speaking countries with a fairly common, though not identical cultural and political value systems, Ayeni breaks new grounds, for which he deserves credit.

By employing the ideological method of analysis, Ayeni brings out the contrasts between political positions that the two candidates staked out and the message systems they used to convey the underlying ideological values that separated them from their opponents. Similarly, a structural analysis enables Ayeni to point out the binary oppositions the campaign messages set up for the candidates and their rivals in terms of values, beliefs and qualities they embodied. In examining verbal codes, Ayeni categorizes the advertising text in groups of speech acts, including representatives (making truth claims, rebuttals and denials) and commissives (in which a candidate makes a commitment to certain causes and promises to deliver on them).

Scrutinizing the discursive, narrative practices used by the candidates to tell their personal tales, Ayeni points out the narrative elements focused on their humble beginnings, love of nation, commitment to service, values and duty in an inspiring way that were designed to generate confidence in the voters.

Ayeni also refers to the issue of the alleged Americanization of the British political campaigns. It was mentioned that the Blair campaign adopted the war room strategy that Clinton had used in his earlier campaign of 1992. Similarities were also noted in the management of information and technology and the use of professional consultants in the two campaigns. But, clearly, ideological affinity between the leaders and the political parties they represented, their personal charisma accentuated by their youthful vigor, futuristic and optimistic approach to solving problems of importance to voters, and empathetic rhetorical styles used in articulating their positions often made the two campaigns look more similar at the macro level than would be justified by a close micro-level scrutiny of the various elements.

Professor Mazharul Haque
University of Southern Mississippi

Acknowledgments

While I acknowledge many people who helped in one way or the other to realize the dream of writing this book, the wholesome responsibility of the contents of the book is entirely mine.

Quite a number of people made the difficult task of putting this book together much easier. I want to use this opportunity to thank Professor Mazarul Haque, who painstakingly worked with me from the very first word to the completion of this book. The idea which came from a doctoral research manifested in a book form years later. I also extend my thanks to Dr. Gene Wigins, Dr. Arthur Kaul, Dr. Wolf and Dr. Tommy Smith.

I'm immensely grateful to my loving family, especially my dear wife, Toyin and my kids, Dapo and Tolu, who were steadfast in their belief in me and stood by me and urged me on during slow times.

I'm indebted to Mike McGarrity of the Democratic National Convention (DNC) who helped with some of the video tapes, the National Democratic Convention (DNC) as well as the British Labour Party for generously providing compilation tapes of the presidential and prime ministerial campaigns in the United States and Britain respectively. Thanks also to Christine Guinerri for thinking up the idea of a title for this book.

Chapter I
Introduction

A comparison of two or more world leaders in terms of their political agendas, tactics or rhetoric is not entirely new in the study of international affairs. It is no less so when the leaders being compared are in charge of two of the world's oldest (George Will, 1991, September 9, *Newsweek*), largest and most popular democracies.

In the past, many similarities have been drawn between world figures like former President Ronald Reagan, the "first TV president", (Griffin and Kagan, 1996) and former British Prime Minister, Lady Margaret Thatcher, in terms of their domestic and international policies, and even their oratorical prowess. Both are successful communicators and ran largely polished professional campaigns. (Semetko et al, 1991, p.16).

Special relationships existed between late President Kennedy and Prime Minister Harold Macmillan just as President Ronald Reagan and Prime Minister Margaret Thatcher shared similar policy postures. (*The Christian Science Monitor*, May, 1, 1997, p.3). Such comparisons have been made easier by television which has provided the center stage where political actors can be scrutinized for special traits like campaign styles, political theatrics, oratorical delivery as well as their "telegenic" looks.

In the case of President Bill Clinton and Prime Minister Tony Blair, the subjects of this research study, the comparison has been so popularly peddled that it is almost being taken for granted. Tony Blair is said to enjoy contradictions like Bill

Clinton, and "both prefer not so much to resolve them as to... "transcend"... them, get around them, ignore them or run right through them." (*New Statesman*, May 1997, p.15). They are believed to possess and share political antics which their opponents lack, and which seemed to have paid off on election days in both countries. They are said to possess the winning formula.

They belong to and share the "baby boomer" image, probably accounting for why they share similar campaign approach, global political and social views, and campaign production techniques. It has been observed that the mantle of world leadership is now resting on the shoulders of the baby boomer generation. (*US News and World Report*, July 25, 1994).

Young Bill and Tony attended Oxford University in England, became lawyers and are married to lawyer wives. Mr. Clinton was said to have further fed the voracious comparisons industry when he telephoned Mr. Blair to congratulate him within minutes of his victory calling it a "terrific win." (*The Economist*, May 10, 1997, p. 56). They enjoy personal friendship as well, a trend which may further lend credence to the general comparison between these young world leaders of the new millennium in terms of their policies and agendas.

A White House aide described the relationship between Blair and Clinton as a "generational bond, having come to power in a post-ideological and post-cold war era." (*Time*, Dec., 8, 1997 p.22). At the party level, an explanation is offered that Mr. Blair never wears a topcoat because his handlers "want to evoke the image of John F. Kennedy, the first politician never to wear a coat while campaigning." (*Maclean's*, May 5, 1997 p. 68). This was to invoke the image of a bouncy and youthful politician, full of vigor rather than the dour look of the older politician he was pitched against.

President Bill Clinton and Prime Minister Tony Blair have been compared at various levels of human accomplishment, perhaps more than any other world leaders in recent history. Levels and aspects of comparison range from general issues like educational attainment, religion, family backgrounds, choice of wives and their profession, and their physical attributes, to such specifics as their shared talents for oratory and political deftness.

To some, Tony Blair is a clone of Bill Clinton, or put crudely, "Tony is Bill without the sex and the sleaze." (*The Economist*, November 9, 1996). While Clinton refers to himself as a "New Democrat", Blair calls his party "New Labor", both tilting the ideological posture of their parties away from the left to the center. (*National Review*, May 6, 1996).

In the 1996-1997 elections in both countries, the fact that Tony Blair and Bill Clinton were pitched against much older, less colorful, and perhaps less vibrant politicians made them not only to shine like stars but hinted at some of the things they may have in common as well. In addition to the environmental factors presented by their opponents, the use of television by Blair and Clinton was to further accentuate the seemingly common grounds between the two politicians.

Therefore, a scholarly analysis to refute or prove any grounds for such comparison has become inevitable for the study of political communication across country and especially for posterity. Hence, this study seeks to identify and analyze perhaps one of the most crucial aspects of democracy, political advertising campaigns, as a means of determining the legitimacy of such comparison. Political advertising is used here loosely since there is a difference in terms of how campaign messages are aired in Britain and in the United States, a situation that calls for definition and explanation of terms in the next section.

Rationale

Political communication is an evolving sub area within mass communication research and education despite the fact that first studies in this area date back to decades ago. It started with the effects of media coverage on voting by Lazarsfeld in 1940. Political communication falls within the realm of messages which have either a remote or direct link with the political discourse. This could include political commercials, campaign speeches, or political debates.

However, due to the wide expanse of political communication research area, this study will focus mainly on a minuscule area known as political advertising. This refers to the short thirty-second campaign commercials that are popular in the United States or the five-to-ten minute Party Election Broadcasts commonly used in Britain. This book compares the content of the political advertising messages during the 1996 presidential elections in the United States and the 1997 General Elections in Britain and provides a general comparison of political communication in both countries. It thus extends beyond political communication to the realm of cross-country research.

Cross-country research provides analysis of issues from different perspectives much more than studies with single issue or single country. Such single-issue studies are often mono-directional in their perspective. This is recurrently so because in comparative analysis, cross-country studies enjoy much richer database, generated from a much broader setting.

The wide nature of the database evidently provides better grounds for generalization than studies with narrower focus. Making comparisons or drawing contrasts help examine events that occurred in different cultural environments. It is, therefore, hoped that there may be a verifiable conclusion that certain traits are common in the most recent communication campaigns used in the United States and British elections. If this happens, it is then likely that an exploration into campaigns in other countries will further deepen our understanding of these processes. This may be especially so in countries which share similar characteristics with the United States and Britain in terms of their political and communication systems.

The general problem in many cross-cultural research studies is the risk of removing events and issues from their natural settings in the process of cross-country data collection and analysis. This may expose cross-cultural studies to misinterpretation and distortion during the research process.

To do justice to a topic that transcends territorial barriers calls for utmost caution so that misjudgments and misrepresentations can be avoided in view of the cultural distance and space. Perhaps the greatest hindrance to most cross-cultural studies of this nature is that of language difference, a problem which, fortunately, does not arise in this study.

The attempt to compare situations in two countries appears to command more legitimacy for identifying contrasting attributes than is the case for comparing situations within a political setting that is already assumed identical. It must be said that not all situations drawn from the same environment end up being identical, and similarities may exist even in cases where two countries are compared. Even though campaign styles of two candidates canvassing for votes in the same country will almost always be different, the sameness of the political setting of the political environment makes them less interesting than comparing two different candidates each from different and political environments.

What this study hopes to achieve is to expand the data base in the area of comparative cross-national political communication and thereby justify or refute the grounds for the generalizations and/or comparisons being drawn from the campaign styles of these two world leaders. The objective here is to ascertain the veracity of the assumption and thus eliminate "naive universalism" and inadvertent "parochialism" (Gurevitch and Blumler, 1990, pp.308-309). This is done by using different research techniques to provide the reader an intellectual verification of the research data gathered for this study.

An analysis of the campaign methods and styles of the two political leaders is done with a view to bringing to the open the areas of similarities and differences in their political communication styles. The issue of whether Bill Clinton and Tony Blair share certain commonalities in communication deserves to be laid bare. This cross-national comparative study will begin by identifying the various features in the political communication styles of the two world leaders, compare such features and determine similarities or differences. This study is envisaged to open new areas of investigation for future comparative studies in political communication, especially in this age of revolutionary landmarks in mass media technology.

An Overview of Media Systems and Elections in the United States and Britain

As a prelude to the main thesis, this book begins by discussing the media systems that operate in both Britain and the United States and identifying the differences in the broadcasting systems of the two countries. This is with a view to understanding the environment and the framework within which the mass media operate in both countries. Such an understanding is necessary in pinpointing why certain things are done differently in both countries and what works in one country and not the other. The broadcast media and indeed political communication in England is run under the guidelines set by the Public Broadcasting Service, with the British Broadcasting Corporation (BBC), created in 1926, as the conduit for political information dissemination.

The British broadcasting system has thrived under what can be categorized as "a duopoly and shared responsibility that has historically supported one of the most stable broadcasting environments in the world." (McNicholas and Ward, 2004, p. 147) The BBC was thus established with the purpose and a duty to inform, educate and entertain. As a corporation run with publicly generated funds, it serves a very crucial role in the democratic process of the country. This is unlike the United States where a fully commercialized broadcast system operates.

Up until 1990 when the Broadcasting Act was enacted, The BBC was wholly financed essentially from television license fee levied annually on television receiver owners. The recent sweeping changes in the structure of broadcasting industry started with the Margaret Thatcher government and competitive structures have been introduced with the diffusion of cable and satellite delivery systems. Despite the changes in the British broadcast media landscape, very little has changed in terms of political communication. As it has always been, political communication through the electronic media costs little or no money to the politicians in Britain.

In covering elections and use of the mass media for political news and information, the guidelines in place are those contained in the Representation of the People's Act 1983 (RPA). Whereas the press seems to have more freedoms as far as election coverage is concerned, broadcast media coverage is guided by strict rules that have seen very few changes since the first recorded party political broadcasts in 1924. (McNicholas and Ward, 2004 p. 151). Most of the laws governing broadcast media coverage are contained in the Broadcasting Act, the Independent Television Commission (ITC), set up to regulate commercial broadcasting, the BBC's Producer Guidelines, and the Radio Authorities (RA) guidelines (for commercial radio stations).

The guidelines on politicians' access to the British broadcast media are stringent, and more controlled than expected, especially as regards paid political advertising. There is an enduring tradition on how time is allocated to political parties for political broadcasts that dates back to the first recorded radio party political broadcasts between the three main party leaders in 1924. This tradition ensures that qualifying political parties are allowed "free access to air time in order that they can convey to the general public party manifestos and party policies." (McNicholas and

Ward, 2004, p. 151).This tradition continues to be honored by the Independent Television Commission (ITC) and its licensed broadcasters. BBC provides this service as part of its public charge to the British subjects.

The newspapers are equally actively involved in election reportage, and are traditionally ideologically slanted in their contents. British newspapers have a national outreach and are also polarized along party lines. In 1997, the Labor Party enjoyed the support of six out of ten major newspapers namely, *The Sun, The Daily Star*, the *Financial Times*, the *Guardian*, the *Independent* and the *Mirror*. The Labor Party was reported to have up to 21.6 million newspaper readers who are members of the party as against the Conservative Party's 10.6 million newspaper readers. The print press was as crucial as the electronic media in the elections of 1997. (Butler and Kavanagh, 1997, p.156). In 2001, the Labor Party was endorsed by 14 daily and Sunday newspapers representing 64 percent of total circulation (McNicholas and Ward, 2004 p. 153)

The print media is less regulated than the broadcast media in Britain, except for issues relating to ownership or defamation of character of public figures, especially politicians. The press operates under the guidelines set by its regulating agency called the Press Complaints Commission, which rarely dangles the long stick except on rare occasions. Any story that puts a politician in the false light with the prospect of affecting the outcome of an election is considered illegal. This is to safeguard politicians from unsubstantiated stories that rival candidates may sell to a newspaper to gain political mileage over the affected politician.

It is important to note that the issue of balance is not an issue in the British media as newspapers ally their stories to whichever party they wish to support. Until recently the Conservatives tended to control more of the newspapers' partisan loyalty and it was argued that this was in tune with the law of economics. The argument is that newspapers rely on advertising and since the Conservative Party supported free trade more than the leftist Labor the support was in place. (McNicholas and Ward, 2004 p. 153). There has been an obvious shift in the last few elections and loyalty seems to be more uncertain for either of the two major parties than before.

In the broadcast media, the polarization was evident in number of party members who watch a particular channel on television. For instance, while BBC share of news coverage of the Conservative Party was about 34.9 percent, it devoted 31.1 for the Labour Party, 21.4 for Liberal Democrats and 9.6 per cent for the others. ITV had 34.6 per cent coverage for the Conservative Party, 24.9, and 27.6 for the Liberal Democrats. C4 had 38 per cent news coverage for Conservatives, 34.3 for Labour and 24.3 for Liberal Democrats. (Butler and Kavanagh, 1997, p.138).

There are special news arrangements in Britain which impact upon the campaigns. One such is the extension of news bulletins to accommodate news from the campaign trail. This does not occur in the United States. However, in the 1997 General Elections in Britain, "the Clintonisation of Labour" (Butler and Kavanagh, 1997, p. 239), was evident. Labor Party's war room concept and the re-direction of New Labour were borrowed from Clinton's 1992 campaign. (p.239). "The professionalization of campaign management and the utilization of modern publicity techniques have had the longest tradition in the United States." (Mathes and Semetko, 1991, p.141).

The relationship between the mass media and the electoral process in the United States has been described as symbiotic. (Kaid and Jones, 2004). The media provide information about the electoral process to the citizenry while the media, whose business is the dissemination of information, serves to spread the word. Information about candidates is largely derived from television coverage despite the vast amount of information sources that abound in the United States. During the 2000 elections, the major networks, CBS, ABC and NBC collectively devoted approximately 52 hours of nightly news programs between January and December spanning the primaries, the campaigns proper and post election period. (Kaid and Jones, 2004).

Just like in Britain, the broadcast media are subject to more rigorous regulatory system than the press. The regulatory body is the Federal Communications Commission (FCC) and its powers are derived from the Federal Communications Act (FCA) of 1934 as revised. The other agency that regulates election issues is the Federal Election Commission (FEC). Key elements of the Federal Communications Act provide that equal access and allowance must be made to all qualified candidates to purchase reasonable amount of air time for the use of the candidate. The equal-time provision, which applies only to federal elections, requires that air time can only be sold at the "lowest unit charge" to the candidates. (p. 32). However, the equal access provision does not extend to issue advertising or party advertising.

The structure of the mass media in the United States is unique. The major networks are crucial in election coverage with Columbia Broadcasting System (CBS), National Broadcasting Company (NBC), and the American Broadcasting Corporation (ABC) being the initial big three. FOX, Warner Brothers Network (WBN) and United Paramount Network have since joined in the competition for wresting audience patronage from the 162 national cable networks. There are also Direct Satellite broadcast providers, and on average each of the cable networks provide 30 or more programs on their channels.

The relationship between the local stations and the networks could be said to be symbiotic in that the local stations that are affiliated to any of the networks distribute programs on behalf of the networks. There is freedom as to how the news stories about elections are covered only to the point where liability claims of falsehood can be instituted by any affected politician. Unlike in Britain, the government does not stipulate requirements for programming only that they operate "in the public interest, convenience, and necessity." (Kaid and Jones, p. 34)

The political parties in the United States do not wield the enormous powers as commonly found in Britain where a Parliamentary system of government is practiced.

In overall comparison with the United States, the British system is a bit more structured in character, clearer in ideology with a higher degree of regional involvement and political party influence. In America, there is less emphasis on party influence but more on individual politicians. The British model has sustained public confidence in political participation and involvement.

In a system-level analysis between Europe and America, it has been noted that there is a stronger multi-party system in Europe than in the United States. Also, that despite the generous use of the media for election campaigns in the United States, turnout is still much higher in Britain or indeed most of Europe. (Mathes and Semetko 1991).

Other areas of differences include the shortness of campaign period in Britain, three to four weeks of intense campaigns, and that of the United States which extends to a period of almost one year. Within this period, two months of intensive campaigns are earmarked solely for the election of the president. The difference in the lengths of campaign period in The United States and Britain has significant impact not just on the news coverage but also on the "dynamics and rhythms of the campaigns in the two countries." (Semetko, et al. 1991, p.12).

In the British Parliamentary system of government the leader of the party with the largest number of Parliament seats becomes the Prime Minister. This hinges the overall electoral success of the Prime Minister on party strength. In the United States, the presidential system of government requires that the president is elected from the list of candidates who emerged from the primaries and the party caucuses. (p.13). As it happens from time to time, control of the legislative houses, that is, the Congress, may be in the hands of the party opposing the president.

Political communication differs in both countries in the area of time allotted to each political party for media campaigns. In the United States emphasis is placed more on individual candidate image and large amounts of money go into 30-second political advertisement spots, particularly on television to boost the candidate's image. However, in the United Kingdom, political parties are allowed free blocks of five-to-ten minutes of air time for Party Election Broadcasts (PEB). (Semetko, et al p.14). The broadcast usually is transmitted between 5:30 p.m. and 11:30 p.m.

Equal air time is made available for purchase in the United States to the parties and contesting candidates. This is subject to availability of funds. Politicians can purchase as much air time as needed and where needed. In Britain, neither the politicians nor the parties can purchase additional air time outside the free block of time allotted to the major parties, even if they had the resources to do so. (Mathes and Semetko, 1991).

The issue of media access has been contentious in the United States as some advocates have argued that less emphasis should be placed on collecting money from sources for the purpose of election campaigns. There have been obstacles on the path of those who look at the British model of free air time for politicians as ideal in that, "any regulations of political campaign processes must be carefully crafted and narrowly focused to avoid conflict with the First Amendment." (Kaid and Jones, p. 41) Money continues to be dominant in American politics and patronage from political party stalwarts provides financial sustenance to parties for their activities especially election campaigns. Soft money contributions have been raised from $1000 to $2000 per election

The structure of political programming on television in the United States is also quite different from that in Britain. This is because the role played by the British Broadcasting Corporation, a public entity, is more beholden to the political structure than that of the United States. In the United States, private ownership of television means stiff competition among television networks. They draw larger segments of the audience through entertainment-oriented programs.

The American networks seem to be more concerned with raising issues involving individual performance of candidates focusing on who is up and who is down at specific points in the campaign. The networks exploited the acrimonious attacks of the candidates on each other as a device to attract audience. On the other hand, the British Broadcasting Corporation even arranges its programming around election campaigns to enable full coverage of electoral issues during the early evening news. In general, campaign coverage is more issue-centered in the United Kingdom than in the United States. (Mathes and Semetko, 1991).

British broadcasting system has gone through a lot of changes from being a social service public-owned enterprise through some sort of liberalization. To compete with the monopoly of the BBC, privately run television stations, "funded by the commercial contractors," were set up. (Smith, 1991, p.47). However, revenue generation, which would have ensured full autonomy, was still tied down to the suppliers of television advertising who took charge of advertising revenue. Channel 4 broke away from this trend only recently after realizing how much this affected revenue base of the organization.

In the United States, television networks and their affiliates share national advertising revenue using an agreeable formula. For instance, the Public Broadcasting System (PBS) which is owned by the publicly-owned depends on financial support from the federal, state and local governments as well as other public donors. Funding in the commercial stations is determined by advertising rates determined by the networks and their affiliates.

Audiences continue to be fragmented due to the incursion of cable networks, Direct Broadcasting System and the Internet. Rupert Murdoch purchased the first satellite system in Europe in the eighties and Britain was a beneficiary with the Sky

Network channels beamed from satellite to viewers' homes. Unlike in America, DBS is still more popular than cable channels in Britain. Also, the type of cross ownership in the media as witnessed in the mass media "empire" of Rupert Murdoch is not allowed in the United States.

Despite the fact that the free air-time allotted politicians to air their campaign messages still remains the exclusive domain of the BBC network, the other channels were reported to have given ample coverage to election news during the last General Elections in Britain. (Butler and Kavanagh, 1997).

Though the differences in the two systems of governments may seem to pose problems of comparison, the ever increasing usage of television, common to both countries, has made such task less daunting, more possible and easy. This is why a study like this one is feasible despite the many differences in the political and communication systems. The use of television has made such comparison possible. Blumler recommends that research in comparative studies should go beyond the rigor of attempting to search for identical features but to also seek to establish equivalencies.

Scope of the study

Due to the systemic differences in the two countries' politics and media systems, it was intriguing to draw parallels from the political campaign messages of Bill Clinton and Tony Blair. This is especially so with the United States' presidential candidate using 30-second spots and the British Labour Party leader employing blocks of between five-to-seven minute long party election broadcasts (PEB). However, since party broadcasts are the exact equivalent of political advertisements in the United States, the comparison was regarded attainable.

Although election campaigns in the two countries did not fall within the same calendar year, they took place a few months apart, and made easy correlation possible. Indeed, a comparison would not have been possible if the campaigns were held at the same time because establishing answers to the question of whether Tony Blair imitated Bill Clinton's styles would have been difficult to attain.

Presidential elections are held in the United States every four years with a maximum of a two-term four-year tenure. Elections may be called anytime within the five-year election interval in Britain. This may be called by the Members of Parliament after a vote of no confidence is passed by the majority. Another process may be by defeating a major government legislative proposal which then forces the Prime Minister to call for a vote of confidence by the House of Commons to assess the popularity of the government. Eurosceptics like John Redwood, Secretary for Wales Affairs in the John Major administration, who stoutly opposed the idea of a united Europe, was one of those who challenged Major to such popularity test at the tail end of the Tory government. To establish any pattern of similarities between two politicians, their election campaign styles stand out as one measure that can give an acceptable conclusion.

Statement of the problem

This book begins on the premise that the comparisons frequently made by the press between these two leaders regarding similarities in their campaign styles are mere assumptions that elicit closer scrutiny using some scholarly research tools. Despite the seemingly challenging barriers posed by geography and distance, international and cross-disciplinary research ought not to be seen as perilous. Rather, it should provide a rich reservoir of valuable information that could be found useful in other societies outside of those two on which the cross-country research is being generated.

Data collected for this study was obtained from recorded video tapes of the political campaigns of Bill Clinton and Tony Blair. They include video tapes of advertising campaigns, party conferences and national conventions speeches as well as literature produced in the form of brochures by the parties' headquarters. It was, therefore, possible to study at various levels the campaign messages and verify claims of similarities or differences between these two leaders. Thus this work falls within the purview of cross-cultural political communication field.

This research study does not seek to measure the political successes or failures of the two subjects in terms of the impact of their campaign messages on their audiences or respective voters. Rather, it sought to compare the various aspects of the campaign messages as a means of identifying differences or similarities that may exist in the ways the politicians campaigned in the last general elections.

This book does not seek to do a comparison of election results; it is not even a comparison of how "Clinton's clone", Tony Blair, was able to influence the British electorate with the imported American strategy. In a study that reviewed election results in both countries, it was found that,

> there has been no correlation of any kind between the results of 13 post-war presidential elections and those of Britain's 14 general elections. Incumbents win, incumbents lose; good candidates do well and bad candidates do badly on both sides of the Atlantic... (*The Economist*, November 9, 1996).

This book seeks to find which aspects of Tony Blair's campaign styles were imitations of those of Bill Clinton.

There is a discussion in the following chapter, right within the section on research questions, on how identified research problems will be solved. In a brief discussion here, the issue of whether there were discernible patterns of campaign messages in terms of narrative styles of the candidates would serve as a crucial link to the other research questions. Do the televised messages have patterns that reflect the political ideologies of the candidates' two parties, and how? The examination of these aspects should go beyond the superficial to determine whether the two leaders' messages were similar both at the level of individual styles and at the party levels. The answers would, therefore, enable students to determine whether there is any connection in the political discourse of the politicians that may have necessitated such widely assumed notion of similarities.

One other very crucial question to be answered is to explore the extent to which the British political campaign styles may have become "Americanized". Since the data relied upon for this book is solely derived from televised political messages, it will be determined how different or similar are the key issue of visual styles adopted. Are there any common characteristics in the textual frames of the campaign messages?

In a general fashion, the book will inquire if there are discernible common traits visible in the political communication patterns of the two leaders that can be generalized in two of the world's most acknowledged democracies. The hypothesis that runs through the whole gamut of this study is that, despite similarities in political cultures of most developed countries that share similar democratic values and hold periodic elections, differences do exist in the ways each country develops its campaign styles. Not uncommon is a trend where one country looks unto the other for ideas on how best to reach their constituents. It is hoped that this will be verified by studying the campaign styles of the two leaders as they used the medium of television to disseminate their messages to the electorate.

Definition of terms: Political advertisement versus
Party Election Broadcast Part Election Broadcast (PEB).

Different political communication styles between United States and Britain pose problems of definition of terms for obvious reasons. This is so because televised political campaigns in Britain do not follow the same pattern as the 30-second political spots commonly used in the United States. However, for the purpose of this study, political campaign messages of the two leaders being compared are analyzed as texts, irrespective of what they are called in the two countries. These messages contained in 30 second commercials of Bill Clinton as well as the four-to-five minute Party Election Broadcasts by Tony Blair are all equated as political campaign messages and are reduced to texts. The objective is to be able to identify significant styles in the texts that merit attention and scrutiny.

In this study, therefore, the reference to the campaign video tapes as political advertisements is avoided because they were produced under different political and media climates. Whereas in the United States as earlier mentioned, parties and individuals pay for air time to convey their advertising messages, in the United Kingdom air time is free, and cannot be referred to as political advertisement.

When a message is framed with the intent to persuade an audience to accept a product or service and positively appraise it, it does not, in of itself, constitute advertising. However, "when the people selling the product pay for time or space to enable them to bring the message in a specific unalterable form to that audience, we call the message advertising." (Jamieson and Campbell, 1997, p.192).

Despite the fact that the objective of the messages aired in both the United Kingdom and the United States before elections was to associate positive image with the candidates and advocate on their behalf for viewers' voting decisions, political messages in the Britain are not called advertisements. They are Party Election Broadcasts (PEB). In the United States, since air time is bought and paid for either by the parties or the candidates, the resultant 30-second spots are referred to as political advertisements.

In this comparative study, the choice of Party Election Broadcasts in the United Kingdom and political ads in the United States was deliberate. This was reinforced by the fact that no parallels could be drawn between the campaign styles of Bill Clinton and Tony Blair without identifying and comparing how they employed the communication tools at their disposal as they reached out to their respective electorate in 1996 and 1997. The political objective of whichever communication tools or styles were employed in both countries is similar even though contrasting electronic media systems in the two countries may have given rise to two different labels. The political broadcasts in Britain and the political campaign ads in the case of United States are thus treated as equivalents of each for the purpose of this textbook.

Political communication which began as an academic discipline in the later part of the twentieth century is a multi-disciplinary discipline incorporating journalism, history, psychology, sociology and rhetoric. It refers to the often-contradictory discourse which is exchanged between political actors, journalists, social commentators, political observers, citizens, or other public opinion makers with a legitimate right to voice their opinions in public on any issue relating to politics. (Walton, 1990, p.12). Kaid (2004) referred to the best and simplest definition of political communication as that provided by Chaffe in his 1975 book which refers to it as, "the role of communication in the political process." Such forms of communication include political advertising, political speeches, debates, or interviews that touch on political issues.

Political spots, campaign commercials or political advertisements refer to those short media messages crafted by political contenders with a view to attracting the attention of a large number of viewers. Political spots contain shots, made up of different scenes, images, texts and audio, such that what is said, and how it is said, helps to create meaning for the viewers. A shot refers to "a continuous take of the camera." (Porter, 1983, p.70) while a scene contains two or more shots. A clip of a video tape is the entire unit of a 30 second campaign. These terms are used frequently in this book to refer to the texts derived from the video tapes. A shot constitutes a shot whether in a 30-second spot or a full-length movie.

Bill Clinton and Tony Blair: A tale of two politicians

A brief but close look at Bill Clinton and Tony Blair provides us with a background to shape our understanding of these often controversial leaders. This will also enable the readers to have an understanding and a feel for the prevailing political situations in the two countries on the eve of the election campaigns of the year covered in the text. This would indicate, in many ways, how campaign issues and messages were framed and this may also explain why certain communication styles and appeals were used to frame the major political issues of that election year.

Perhaps, an understanding of these men and their histories will make it possible to explain the links between their social and political beliefs prior to the campaigns, their election campaign styles and their campaign narratives. Such a social and political framework helps to define each person's personality as well as how they communicate through their narratives. Individual's narrative styles are closely linked to their histories and backgrounds. This is especially so because narratives are said to be "the principle by which people organize their experience, knowledge about, and transactions with the social world." (Bruner, 1990, p. 35).

Tony Blair became leader of the British Labour Party in May, 1994 following the sudden death of the former party leader, John Smith. Thereafter, on assuming the leadership of the party, he embarked on the continuing "process of programmatic and organizational "modernization" that Smith and Neil Kinnock, his predecessors, had started." (Webb, 1996, p. 482). He was seen as the "harbinger of a whole new kind of European politics, a twenty-first century politics." (*Foreign Affairs*, March/April, 1997)

In a rather ambitious fashion, he proceeded to reform Clause Four, the bedrock of the Labor Party's socialist beliefs, arguing that he wanted to

"reinvent the left," an explanation many thought was not just unacceptable but impossible. Clause 4 assured British citizens of securing for the workers by hand or by brain the full fruits of their industry, and the most equitable distribution thereof that may be possible, upon the basis of common ownership of the means of production, distribution and exchange. (*Foreign Affairs*, March/April, 1997 p.45).

Tony Blair promised the British people a "dynamic economy... a just society...an open democracy...a healthy environment." (*Foreign Affairs*, p.46). He left no one in doubt that the Labour Party was not going to be the same again. He had replaced Labour's socialism with what he called the "stakeholder economy". (p.47)

Clinton and Blair assumed leadership of their countries following prolonged conservative rule. In Britain, the Tories had been in power for 18 years while following Jimmy Carter's defeat by Reagan in 1980, the Republicans had been in the White House for 12 years. Clinton broke the 12-year cycle of Republican control of the presidency just as Blair ended the 18-year-Tory rule in Britain.

Capitalizing on their youthful looks and charisma, both began a course of reshaping their parties' platforms. The buzzwords in their slogans were small government, no taxes, pro-growth and pro-business. Clinton deviated from the Democratic Party norms by focusing on deficit cuts, and free-trade agreements. In Britain, Blair made the Labor Party shed its anti-business image by espousing free trade, and steering the party away from using the word "socialism". (*Maclean's*, May 5, 1997, p. 68).

Blair sent top officials of his party to the Democratic Party's convention in Chicago from which the crucial lesson of wooing Britain's middle class voters was learned. John Prescott, deputy party leader, was quoted as saying that Labour's victory was hinged upon the middle class segment of the electorate being converted into the Labour fold. (*Christian Science Monitor*, September 3, 1996, p. 6). In addition, purposeful policies, based on family values, fiscal conservatism and toughness on crime were vigorously used to rally support.

On taking over power in 1997, Blair, at age 43, was the youngest Prime Minister of Britain in the twentieth century. Tony Blair is the second Prime Minister of Britain in history to have a "secure majority" assuring the Labor Party of their first victory in 23 years and the greatest victory ever. (National Executive Committee Report, 1997, p.4). He learned that the crucial issue of an economically united Europe was the Achilles' heel for John Major, his predecessor in office and he sought to make a "fresh start" on Europe. (*Europe*, May 1997, p. 25). His dream for his party was to make it a "modern professional fighting force", (p. 25), possibly one capable of weathering any future Tory attacks.

Tony Blair recruited new 75,000 converts in the year before elections and wrote a report, *Listening to Women,* with a view to appeasing women voters. He introduced a new lexicon of words into the political discourse of the Labor Party. He is famous for facing confrontations headlong.

Son of a law professor, Tony Blair's father had planned to run for British parliamentary elections as a conservative before he became disabled due to a serious stroke (*Time*, Apr., 28, 1997, p.48). Just as Clinton went through rigorous campaigns, in search of strayed democrats who, swayed by Reagan rhetoric, had repeatedly brought back the Republicans into office, Blair brought back lost Labour voters to the Labour fold. (p.49). He began this by steering his party away from the traditional leftist ideological position to the center, a trend that was also becoming popular in all of Europe. (p.49).

Mr. Blair sought the cooperation of the Liberals and he endorsed the idea of a referendum on electoral reforms especially concerning Wales, Scotland and Northern Ireland. The Liberal Democrats, the third most popular party, warmed up to this agenda. On the run off to the elections he led his opponent and incumbent John Major by more than 20 points in opinion polls.

Many prominent Conservatives cashed in on Major's weak leadership by defecting to either the Labour Party or the Liberal Democratic Party. (Webb, 1996, p. 484). Rumors of "sexual peccadilloes and pecuniary corruption." (p. 484) furthered the public's lack of confidence in the Tory government. Members of Parliament were also accused of taking money from people to raise issues in the House of Commons that favored them or their business interests. Any leftover chances of the Tories to stay in power thinned as elections drew closer.

What is really most exciting about a comparative study of campaign styles of Clinton and Blair is that John Major, Blair's predecessor in office, was enmeshed in as many crises as Bill Clinton on the eve of the elections. Although John Major was seen as "innocent John", it was his sexually wayward and dissenting cabinet members that put a hole in Tory's political roof. One of the Members of Parliament (MP) had an affair with a 17-year-old nightclub girl while another one was accused of extorting money from an influence purchaser who sought to buy favors from the House of Commons. Tony Blair took control with 179-seat majority in the House of Commons.

It was surprising how these crises catapulted Major out of office while Bill Clinton, bidding for a return to the White House, even though it appeared his crises were of greater magnitude than Major's, was still able to win the elections in America. What Clinton shared with John Major in terms of political crises was neutralized by his great communication prowess.

When the 104th Congress convened on January 4, 1995, the Republicans had majority in both the Senate and the House of Representatives for the first time since 1954. Riding on the crest of the popular agenda of the time, "Contract with America", the Republicans were gunning for the White House. The sweeping changes contained in the rhetoric of the new right wing conservatives who had just taken over the United States Congress appeared poised to claim Clinton as a casualty.

"The Contract" called for a "balanced budget, constitutional amendment and line-item veto, criminal law reforms, welfare reforms, reforms dealing with family and children, tax cut for the middle class among other items. (Webb, 1996, p. 489). Clinton countered the Contract with his own agenda in which he called for "a new covenant between the people and the government, an increase in minimum wage, tax credits for higher education, gradual health care reform, campaign finance, and an overhaul of welfare system." (p. 490).

Despite President Clinton's seemingly intractable scandals, he was able to claim victory over Senator Bob Dole, a seasoned politician with an impeccable and unimpeachable character both in public and private lives. At a personal level both Clinton and Blair were faced with competition from politicians, Bob Dole in the case of Clinton and John Major in the case of Blair, whose strong points included sterling character qualities.

While Clinton, as incumbent, was able to tide over the crises that engulfed him before the elections, John Major, also an incumbent, was unable to survive in Britain. Euroskeptics within the ranks of the Tory Party became thorns in the Tory Party balloon boosting Blair's soaring political image and bursting the bubbles for the Tories. (*The American Spectator*, June 1997 p. 86)

For most of the campaign period, Clinton kept the lead in the opinion polls. This was in spite of Bob Dole's frequent references to Clinton's moral lapses in most of his campaign. For instance according to one of the many polls, Dole's campaign spots seemed to have a positive impact on his image in September of 1997 but a few weeks later in October, just close to the election, the tide changed positively to Clinton's advantage. (Kaid, 1997).

Clinton used the incumbency factor, hinging his campaign messages more on his record in office which included a better economic climate, more police to combat crime, a stable foreign policy, better schools, keeping guns off the streets. These messages worked against the hawkish image of the GOP's.

The stalemate that resulted from the controversy on a balanced budget further enhanced the negative impact on the credibility of the Republican Party. The Republicans were portrayed as anti-senior citizens especially because of their insistence on pursuing policies in the Congress that were perceived to have negative consequences on the interests of the senior citizens. Bob Dole's campaign machinery played into the hands of Clinton supporters, who succeeded in roping in Bob Dole, despite his sterling qualities, with the rest of the "GOP Gang" in the Congress. Through a calculated tactic of demonizing the Republicans, fear was created in the electorate that the Republicans could not be trusted, Clinton's record of sex scandals not withstanding.

Clinton and Dole were thus embroiled in a battle for recognition, and as Devlin (1997) noted, the 1996 election was the most costly, and involved the highest-spending advertising campaign ever. Although it was issue oriented, it was the most negative campaign in the history of presidential campaign spots. (Kaid, 1998).

It is perhaps appropriate to mention some of the qualities shared by Clinton's and Blair's opponents in the elections as this might explain why some of the campaign styles adopted by Blair and Clinton are similar or different. Bob Dole, the Republican candidate for president, was seen as an impeccable old politician almost too good for the twenty-first century America. Indeed despite opinion-poll results which indicated that more Americans would trust their children with Bob Dole, it was quite intriguing as to why they did not vote for him on the day of election.

John Major, Tony Blair's opponent in the British General Elections, was seen as the surrogate to Margaret Thatcher. John was the innocent one, who was unfortunately surrounded by wayward cabinet members who would stop at nothing to sink Major's abandoned and desolate political ship. Many faithful party supporters had defected while those within continued to wage campaigns against him on his policies on the European Union. Clinton revived the undying Kennedy enigma, that of a youthful leader on whom voters were ready to stake their loyalty and support.

In a similar vein, the British electorate saw a variant of Clinton in Tony Blair, at least to have their turn of the Kennedy "myth" re-enacted in their own Tony Blair. He was the youngest Prime Minister in 200 years. Polished and not short of words, nor unskilled in how to use them very well to his advantage, Blair conveyed the image of a youthful leader on whom the voters were eager to stake their trust instead of the tested and trusted John Major. What then did Bill Clinton and Tony Blair do that made them eventual winners in their countries?

Research Questions

This study proposed to examine and analyze the campaign messages of these two leaders and find answers to the following categories of research questions:

(1) Communication acts and Linguistic codes:

In a series of questions with the main focus on comparing the communication acts of the two leaders, the following research questions were posed:

> (a) Were the narrative styles used by the leaders similar? This explores whether there is any closeness in the structure, themes, plot, tone and pitch of the messages. It compares how the two leaders tell their stories and with what.

> (b) Were there any connections in the political discourse of the politicians? Discourse here will examine whether there were specific qualities discernible in their argumentation and story-telling styles. This examined how the leaders used language not just as speakers but as members of social categories, groups, professions, organizations,

societies or cultures. (p.3). It is the discourse that shapes the many properties of the socio-cultural situation called context.

(c) Did the two leaders use similar verbal codes? This will explore how each of them used attitudinal, valuative and metaphorical language. Attitudinal language refers to words used to express positive or negative judgments about the other candidate. (Berg, Wenner and Gronbeck, 1998, p.96). Valuative language explores what sociological, moral, psychological, religious or aesthetic codes are embedded in the messages. Metaphorical use of language occurs when situations or events are described with something else that adds value and meaning to what is being described.

(2) Did the leaders share similar ideological frames?

This question will explore if the messages reflected the political ideologies of their two parties. This will address the party platforms of both parties, the Democratic Party in the United States and Labour Party in the United Kingdom. Both parties that traditionally espoused leftist political ideals seem to have moved to the center of the ideological spectrum in the nineties. How did the messages of the two leaders reflect this ideological shift?

(3) Visual Codes:

(a) Which visual styles were used? In other words, the study identified the locations, settings, symbolic icons and rhetorical genres to detect similarities or differences. Did the leaders, especially at the semiotic level, use common signs in their campaign messages? Signs here mean "everything that, on the grounds of a previously established social convention, can be taken as something standing for something else." (Eco, 1976, p.16).

(b) Were there common textual frames in the campaign video? Textual frames describe the ways "the experience was organized to convey a particular definition of reality" (Morreale, 1991 p. 6).

(c)What were the positions of the candidates in each frame? How did objects in the background and the foreground complement each other?

(d) In addition to identifying the frames, using the ideology as a frame or definition of reality, the question examines the myths used and the way they were communicated. Which types of myths were invoked by the campaign messages?

(4) Production techniques:

(a) How did color presentation augment the meanings embedded in the video shots? Did the lighting assist in adding to or detracting from the meanings?

(b) What was the interaction between verbal, visual and acoustic codes? How did the interaction help to augment meaning making process?

(5) Americanization/Globalization of campaign styles:

(a) How "Americanized' was the British political campaign messages? Kaid et al, (1991) identified "heightened emphasis on candidate image, instead of party loyalties" (p.1) as key features of the American politics, the sharp, pungent sound bites, otherwise called "capsulated messages', imported from United States, (Day, 1982, p.8) became common in the United Kingdom as well. The Americans supposedly, exported the technique of commercial marketing of politics to Britain in 1970 at the behest of the Conservative Party.

The research question on the Americanization of political campaign styles is important because it has been said time and time again that American consultants and politicians are exporting election styles and technology to other countries of the world. There is indeed almost an irresistibly alluring myth surrounding the great influencing power of United States election campaign practices. (Swanson and Mancini, (1996). It has been copied in the least expected places like Russia where President Boris Yeltsin used the campaign war room style as well as focus group sessions to devise campaign strategy. Is the British election campaign copying the American style?

Chapter II
Review of the Literature

Political communication is perhaps one of the more active areas of research in communication field. From the seminal work of Lazarsfeld, Berelson and Gaudet (1948) to agenda-setting role of communication on voter perception, research work has veered into newer areas of inquiry spanning a wide expanse of disciplines and issues, especially due to the important role of television in politics. There have been many diverse theoretical frameworks used in political communication research over the years ranging from media effects to agenda setting, diffusion of news events, and use of new communication technologies.

The dramatic way in which modern communication technology, especially television, changed the nature of political communication has enabled research study in the area of advertising effects to thrive over the years. The ability of television to reach a wide range of audiences with political advertising messages makes its role in politics very significant. Interest was sparked in political advertising research by the development of a transactional model of communication, which opened up new frontiers of variables likely to be swayed by political advertising. A transactional model of communication signaled to researchers that media use often resulted in negotiated meaning.

Moving on from the media-effects research, which established that political advertising does have effect on its audience, attention shifted in the mid-1970's to assessing the variables that measure the impact of political advertising on audience. Many types of effects were also identified in political communication literature

31

during the period. These included literature with focus on selective exposure, awareness and knowledge, agenda-setting or candidate preference and those that examined the influence of advertising on election outcome and voting levels.

In the area of assessing the content of political advertising messages, extensive work was done on production techniques, issue presentation by the candidates, appeals, and styles used. The review of literature for this study incorporated studies done in the area of comparative analysis of political advertising as well as those that touch on globalization of campaign techniques.

The review of these studies was, therefore, divided into categories with each section dealing with the themes common to all the research work in that group. These include:

(1) Advertising effects/impact on voter attitude.

(2) Advertising content research dealing with analysis of political advertising content.

(3) Research with focus on advertising styles, including production techniques.

(4) Research work with focus on "Americanization" or globalization of advertising campaign, and

(5) Research work on comparative political communication across cultures.

Considerable amount of work has been done with specific focus on the impact/effect of political communication on audience reaction to political messages. Chanslor (1996) studied the impact of campaign messages on voter behavior. It is often argued that political campaign messages do influence voter perception of candidates. Studies like those by Patterson and McClure (1976); Jamieson (1984); Diamond and Bates (1984) and Biocca (1991) focused on spot advertisements and their place in American political culture. (Morreale, 1996).

On the other hand, McCombs and Gilbert (1986) place emphasis on agenda setting processes, while Nimmo and Combs (1990) deal with the symbolic construction of the political candidates' identities. An earlier work on political symbols was done by Edelman (1964) and Elder (1983) in which political symbols were identified as playing significant roles in campaign rhetoric.

Edelman and Elder argue that symbols are used as rallying point for support from groups of people who share similar fears and anxieties, and they see the symbols as a means of reassurance for their "group identity, life style or set values." (p.17) Symbols constitute the rallying point for all those who share similar fears and anxieties and who see themselves represented by those symbolic images.

Jamieson (1986) provided a historical guide to the political advertising research by identifying those features that have changed over the years in campaign communication methods. He reminisced over the pre-television era of the torchlight parades of the mid-19th century and discussed the dynamic changes that are present today through the proliferation of political campaign consultants and media technology. The use of modern interactive communication technologies in political communication especially in its use for resolving social problems was identified by Rogers (2004). He refers to the setting up of Public Electronic Network (PEN) with the objective to encourage interactive exchange of ideas among the people and to trigger political mass participation.

Devlin (1986) identified different types of political advertisements. These include documentary film, man-in-the-street, testimonial or independent advertisements. (p.29). Politicians choose some or all of these categories depending on the scope of their campaigns. Studies by Cundy (1986), and Meadow and Sigelman (1982) established a relationship between advertising and voter perception while Nowlan and Moutray (1984) explored the link between advertising messages acting as catalyst for winning votes. These studies reinforced the notion that advertising furthered the chances of a victory for any politician who exploited it to the maximum.

It was, however, found out by Garramone cited in Swanson and Nimmo, 1990), that the audience could be "primed" so as to ensure that they get the desired motivation toward the ads. Increasingly, recent studies have shown that a backlash effect of negative ads on the sponsor of the ads has surfaced. Rather than result in negative voter perception for the target candidate, the candidate initiating the negative advertising were found to be hurt more by such negativity. (Garramone, 1984; Merrit, 1984).

The common flaws identified in some of these works which centered solely on audience attitude to political advertisements were that they failed to record and analyze the significant factor of meaning. This is so particularly since all the analysis of advertising effects stopped short at the crucial stage of message analysis. They failed especially by not effectively capturing the candidate's style, rhetoric or even delivery method.

It is valuable to measure the impact created by political advertising messages on the audience as has been done in some of these studies earlier mentioned. However, critics of the impact/effect studies of political campaigns on audience argue that the impact of the message cannot be effectively measured without analyzing what is contained in the messages. The analysis of the content of political advertising provides a deeper level of understanding and an explanation beyond what an impact/effect study could.

Political advertising content literature

Kaid and Holtz-Bacha (1995) edited a collection of political communication literature by dividing them into groups incorporating content and styles, effects, and comparisons across cultures. A follow up to that was done by Kaid (2004) in which the categories identified include Issues versus image literature, newspaper and print advertising content, and negative versus positive ads.

Holtz-Bacha and Kaid (1991) coded 67 spots, 2.5 minutes in length, from 21 parties during the 1990 campaigns in Germany. Some of the categories coded included documentary, issue presentation, testimonial, production techniques, and candidate statements, among others. These categories were content analyzed. Part of the results showed that there were differences in the evaluations of the candidates by East and West Germans. This was linked to the differences in their political background.

Joslyn (1986) expanded the comparison of image and issue content in political advertising. This revealed the purposes that elections hold for voters and how they make their voting decisions. The study found out that advertising campaigns in the United States were issue centered not policy-oriented.

Visual characteristics of spots were studied by Shyles (1984b) while verbal and non-verbal methods and production styles were examined by Kaid and Davidson (1986). However, it was Kaid's (1981) study that linked political advertisement contents to cognitive, affective and behavioral effects on voters. It was indeed a marked improvement on the research studies that focused solely on message impact.

An interesting addition was the analysis of color in campaign videos in which Williamson (1993) found that there was a basis for connection or connections unstated by the verbal part of the advertisement and the colors in which they were presented. Colors, in association with words, supposedly tell stories, and in unity provide depth in our interpretation of the message intended. Political communication being a terrain where images are as crucial as the presentation styles employed, the role of color in image presentation and enhancement is important.

Television packs the dual advantage of audio and video qualities that serve very unique purposes for politicians. Combined with these are non-static pictures, through which we are able to add the significant role of color, or lack of it, in our overall assessment of the message being conveyed. In essence, therefore, colors play a vital role in television advertising campaigns. The visual effects of image enhancement, provided by colors add a compelling impact that attract and arrest viewers' attention.

Leland (1991) presented a qualitative analysis of political campaign messages. Using a triangulation technique of research, he applied a combination of descriptive, analytical and comparative methods to his analysis of political campaigns. This was done by providing a description of narrative form, how a narrative develops, narrative styles, and how narrative themes are discovered. In addition, he discussed the theoretical implications of "narrative functionality." (DAI-A 52/06).

Griffin and Kegan (1996) differed in their study which called for a deeper level of visual analysis that focuses on the salient cultural images which reside in the messages. To them, visual effects become very important when they are able to bring to the fore, those cultural aspects that further lend meanings to the messages being conveyed. Those identified cultural images are, "depiction that makes reference to national, regional, ethnic, religious, sub-cultural archetypes, and historical associations." (p.45). These can be located in what he calls the "mise en scene" or the production scenery, settings, backdrops, within the video frame.

Cultural symbols like flags, national monuments, or other historic features and artifacts that bind a people as a nation constitute a part of what is known as the "montage". They provide deep-seated meanings to scenes in the messages. Viewers are able to associate meanings to them even without any reference to them in the text. In a comparative analysis, Griffin and Kegan (1996) explore those visual symbols with cultural significance that can be located in the American and Israeli prime ministerial elections of 1992.

They proceed from the fact that political spots are not just "discrete, rhetorical maneuvers," (Jamieson, 1989), to unravel the "contextual meanings" of the political advertisements. Their approach began with a shot-by-shot analysis of features of images that were identified as having cultural import and then drawing comparisons and contrasts between spots form Israel and America.

They looked at vignettes or, "sequences of brief images used to symbolize people from different walks of life," (p.49), and concluded that the comparison of the images served to "sensitize us to the importance of cultural images in political myth making and rhetoric." (p.58).

Joslyn in two separate studies (1984, 1986) used content analysis method and expanded the comparison of image and issue content to reveal the purpose which elections hold for voters and how they make their voting decisions. His summation was that usually, voters based their voting decisions on prior knowledge of the leadership styles and image qualities of the candidates.

He also found that 63 percent of the spots contained facts which were helpful in voters' choice for either a change or continuity, 57 percent included candidate image content while only 15 percent focused on issues. This indicated that voters depend considerably on television spots for information on which they based their voting decisions.

In another study, West (1994), examined television spots from 1972 to 1990 and combined 16 public opinion surveys (panel and cross-sectional) used to investigate viewers' reactions to campaign advertisements. He also looked at *New York Times, Washington Post* and *CBS Evening News* in his study in a combination of research approach that incorporated experiment with public opinion surveys.

Eight hundred and eighty three randomly selected respondents were interviewed on the phone, 261 newspaper articles were also studied. Four-point ad-viewing scales were used to measure exposure and frequency or attentiveness of viewing. In conclusion, West found that the best predictors of voters' decision on a candidate's electability depended on exposure to political spots.

The use of negative ads in politics detracts from the important issues for politicians to focus on, and the outcome of such negative use of ads has been a popular research area. It has been confirmed that negative ads do have a backlash effect on the sponsor of the negative message. (Jasperson and Fan, 2002; Sonner, 1998; and Lemert, Wanta and Lee, 1999). Kaid (1997) studied the television spots of Bob Dole and Bill Clinton in the 1996 elections for president. Using experimental method, she investigated the effects of technological distortions on the images of Clinton and Dole. The goal of the study was to find out whether such distortions affected voter perception negatively or otherwise.

The importance of this study stemmed from the fact that the 1996 presidential elections, besides the huge cost, reached an all-time high in distortions. About 70 percent of the entire campaign spots, 84 percent of Clinton's and 49 percent of Dole's were identified to be in that category. Kaid found out that the distortions in the spots were not only effective, but respondents were more likely to respond negatively to such distortions.

During the 2004 elections, issues were once again relegated to the back burner while negative ads took prime spots in the media. The issue was about John Kerry, the Democratic Party nominee for president, who has been on the receiving end of negative ads that question his military service during the Vietnam War. While George Bush's campaign camp denied knowledge of the smear attack, the said negative ad has not been condemned.

Negative ads rely on distortions, and such distortions which may be visual or verbal are better done with the application of visual effects that tended to place the opposing candidate in less than attractive position when compared to the originating candidate. Color, camera angles, even distorted audio, selective quotes which were taken out of context, could all add up to make or mar candidates' political image or even the entire campaigns. The fact that opinion polls did not change in favor of Bob Dole despite the negative advertising campaign spoke volumes for the effect of negative campaign on the initiating candidate.

Despite what may be said about negative political ads, strange as it may sound, it should be noted that they tend to be more issue-oriented than positive ads. (Kaid 2004). There is higher level of recall for negative ads exposed to voters than there is for positive ads. (Kahn and Kenney, 2000). Negative ads are said to increase accuracy and speed of visual recognition (Newhagen and Reeves, 1991). Negative ads trigger knowledge of issues and ability to better evaluate candidates for voters who recall such negative ads. (Brians and Wattenberg, 1996).

Studies that employed qualitative methods of research in political communication are few and far between. This is why Marvin (1994) in his analysis of the 1992 presidential election stands out. He employed an anthropological style for the interpretation of campaign messages. He likened the American election to a ritual of some sort and proposed an analysis of the 1992 elections based on Marcus and Fischer's (1986) traditional ritual analysis.

He approximated the whole election process to one huge celebrated ritual, incense burning, blood splitting, sacrifices and all other features common in grand rituals. The relatedness that he locates between the themes of killing, feasting, sacrifice for a group's nourishment, regeneration and existence in presidential elections is striking. It is interesting to note that primaries, political campaigns and national conferences of parties have become huge events in the age of ritualistic celebrations!

Rather than embark on an "outcome oriented study" which asks why candidate "A" won or why he did not, (Nimmo and Swanson, 1990), Marvin (1994) analyzed features of elections as they present themselves. According to him, features we generally assumed to be problems in our political culture, like negative campaigns, may be a part of the surviving elements that identify us and serve as our "group solidarity." Therefore, dirty campaigns or negative advertisements may "not be evidence of social pathology after all, but a constitutive feature of American civic ritual." (p. 266).

To Marvin (1994), campaign period is when the candidates are "tortured and brutalized to be served up to a rapacious and devouring electorate," (p. 267) while horse race in elections is likened to the mating of two fertile pairs, the victorious candidate and the electorate. The inauguration represents "the christening of the chosen "son", the dedication of a promised child conceived in the fertility of the election." (p.282).

Suggesting that elections and their accompanying rituals are embedded in a people's political culture, Marvin's study takes our attention off the quantitative approach to political communication, which makes the whole perspective abstract, by placing us within the context of a social norm that requires critical-cultural analysis to appreciate.

After all, according to Marvin, the two candidates are similar to the sacrificial goats used in Leviticus. While the winner takes upon himself the sins of the people and goes into the wilderness, the loser is selected for immediate killing. (p.288). The political metaphors applied here are apt description of the pains and pangs associated with contesting elections, and while the winner takes on the people's problems by providing nourishment and survival instinct to the community, the loser often wanders into political oblivion, or "death." Only very rarely do they ever make a come-back.

Political advertising styles

The notion that television has provided a center stage for political actors, who play to the gallery, can be aptly demonstrated by looking at how campaign styles have been transformed from being a means of talking to your audience to an art of addressing spectators. It is no longer what you say to your spectators but how well you say it. No wonder, therefore, that production styles in campaign communication is as important, if not more important, than what is being communicated. Under the circumstance, all known techniques that serve to enhance communication are put to use. Color arrangement, voice inflection, mode of dressing, settings, even hair styles, all combine to help the "actors" look better in how they are presented.

Using color in political ads adds value to how we tell a story and provides "oral connection" between objects, the world and the person. (Williamson, 1978, p.22). In its most effective use color serves to make correlation between objects or images, for example, between a product and other related things for distinction. Most importantly, color can be effectively used to make differentiation by making one thing stand out while making the other stick out like a sore thumb.

Even beyond color analysis, studies have shown that minor camera angle adjustments may stimulate major differences in perceptions of advertising messages, especially in influencing the homogeneity of the perception of the speaker. (Kepplinger and Donsbach, 1987). Saint-Martin's (1990) semiology of visual language breaks visual images down to components made up of color, texture, dimension, boundaries, vectorality and position in the plane. All these combine to unite in what she refers to as the coloreme, or the most basic or minimal unit of visual language.

Murray and Murray (1996)'s examined the impact of music in commercials. They referred to Bruner's (1990) study by observing that despite the common usage of music in almost all commercials, out of the 20 studies that looked at music in advertisements up until 1990, not one focused on lyrics. Most of them, they noted in their study, dealt with aspects such as texture, pitch, tempo, etc. (p.51). However, it was Gorn's (1982) study on the global effects of music on behavior that noted that, an unconditioned stimulus was bound to invoke an unconditioned response. In other words, music served a vital role in activating a type of response from the audience by enhancing meanings that may otherwise be absent without it. (p. 52).

Morreale (1991) uses a televisual rhetorical criticism in a textual frame analysis to interpret Ronald Reagan political message, "A new beginning." This work makes use of insights from "contemporary film criticism, television criticism, politics and cultural studies." (p. 5). She observed that meanings are socially constructed, and that we define our world through the use of symbols which are multi-vocal in their production of meanings. An explanation is provided on how framing helps in the interaction of context, source, text and audience leading to the production of meanings. (p. 96).

Morreale insists that a study must include an analysis of images so as to be able to answer the questions, are these images populist, or are ordinary people lending their voices to the campaign messages? Also, are there proxy narrators through whose mouths the image of the candidate is being projected? Do the candidates use visual clichés of symbolic value like flags, national monuments, farms, and other symbols that encourage nationalistic feelings? The author also indicates that background songs and musical note should form core objects of analysis. She identified highly stylized images that may or may not be chronologically synthesized.

The author was thus able to determine if the scenes were issue-centered or whether the overall tone of the film was lighthearted and laden with visual techniques and other production styles that distinguished the messages. This style, called the textual frame analytic approach is unique in the way it focuses on stylistics of campaign videos and explains how context, source, text and the audience interact.

Reinforcing the fact that meaning resides not in just the spoken words but also within the context and environment in which they were used Biocca (1991) provides a succinct explanation about messages, context and meaning. In his study, he asks us to decompose advertisements into words, images and sounds for the purpose of looking for the units of meaning within them. (p.19). It is in such units of meaning that we find the signs that form the elements that convey meanings. Biocca (1991) breaks video segment into units comprising words, non-verbal gestures, static images and sounds that combine to provide full meanings to messages. (p.19).

This holistic approach confirms the reasoning that meanings within political advertisements reside not just in what is said but as much as what is not said, but are portrayed in other communicative forms that are non-verbal. Sweaty forehead, nervous movements, shuffling or shifting on a chair, fidgety movements of hands, and other involuntary acts can sometimes send messages that are outside of the text but still add significant meanings to the overall picture all the same.

All of these acts are significant even when the candidates are filmed under identical situations or even in a scene where face-to-face questions are posed to them. A ready example is the political debate setting. There are still noticeable differences that can be observed not just in the way the candidates answer the questions but also how television portrays them. Although years ago when Maxwell and Shaw (1979) conducted their studies on how television affects viewers' images of candidates, they noted that research in that area was "inconclusive and contradictory", that cannot be said to be the case today.

Kepplinger and Donsbach (1987) observed that the position of the camera during the filming of a scene could lend extra meaning to the scene or detract from it. They noted that, "conceivably minor adjustments in camera angles may stimulate major differences in audience perceptions of candidates." (p.70). For instance, camera positions during the Nixon/Kennedy debate is often referred to as a veritable evidence on how camera position can make or mar candidate image based on audience perceptions.

Kraus (1996) in a study re-exposed a select audience to the often-mentioned Nixon-Kennedy debates to assess the better candidate of the two. The post-test rated the candidates based on their perceptions. In the results, more subjects agreed that Kennedy won the television debate while Nixon was adjudged the winner of the radio debate. In many studies that have been done on the Nixon/Kennedy debate, Kennedy was adjudged better because he used television more effectively to his advantage.

What makes Kraus' study significant is the fact that the same subjects that adjudged Kennedy better in the televised debate said Nixon was better on radio, an indication that television effects may have influenced their decisions on the TV debate. This served to affirm that the way a candidate was presented had a vital role to play on how they were rated by the voters/audience.

In a similar study, Rosenberg and McCafferty (1987) experimented by using hypothetical candidates to find different evaluations in the candidates based on the judgment of the viewers. They did this by "varying the facial expressions in the photos" of the candidates. (p.303). Rosenberg, Kahn and Tran (1991) were able to influence voters by manipulating the facial features of female candidates. (p.303). A study of the 1976 German election showed that television coverage especially camera positioning placed Helmut Schmidt at an advantage over Helmut Kohl just by filming Schmidt from a better camera angle. (p. 303).

McHugo et al (1985) also found that eye-level shots tended to portray candidates being filmed in a favorable light more than those not filmed from that angle. All of these tended to support the notion that pictorial representations do affect and influence public opinion and attitudes toward a candidate. (p.304)

In another experiment to prove the importance of production techniques in political campaigns, Kepplinger and Densbach (1987) exposed viewers to films of political shots which were produced using different camera angles. After exposure to this stimulus, their perceptions of the speaker were compared in a post-test.

The results showed that camera angles inconsistently influenced the tendency of perception of individual characteristics. It was also found that the influence was more significant with the supporters than neutral voters or opponents. (p. 67). The way the candidate is portrayed through the delivery of camera angles could thus be said to be potent in swaying supporters away from a candidate if the effect on them is considered negative. In other words, camera angles have influence on the "homogeneity" of the perception of the speaker. (p. 71).

In the analysis of texts in political campaigns, researchers must be aware of those features that need be identified for analysis. How do we identify those segments of the text that require attention? Which segments warranted deeper attention' And how do we ensure that in seeking to identify meaning carrying segments, we are not ignoring salient issues contained in the messages? These answers are provided in the following studies.

The studies by Chafe (1974), and Clark and Clark (1977) are relevant here because they showed how to segment texts into frames for the purpose of analysis. They defined frames of meaning as "the opening phrase of a sentence which orients the processing and which the rest of the text further constrains." (Biocca, 1991, p.37).

Without identifying the frames, attempting to isolate all the codes inherent in a message as well as its signs could pose tedious. Video frames can be easily determined by merging all the codes and signs they contain into semantic frames, or a unit that conveys meaning to the viewer. Semantic frame is defined as the "textual or message strategy for the cultivation of desired schema in the mind of the viewer." (Biocca, 1991, pp.37-38).

In another study, Biocca (1991) approached his analysis of political advertising video tapes from a microscopic level. This involves breaking video segment into units made up of words, non-verbal gestures, static images, and sounds all of which "allow for breaking into the units of meaning in the advertisements." (p.18).

Reissman's (1993) narrative approach argues that, "telling stories is a universal human activity" and a way we make sense out of other people's experiences. Denotative and connotative meanings, words, striking features, nuances, movements, and other para-linguistic aspects of the message can be identified to lend full meaning to the story being narrated.

This is shared in the works of Tannen (1993), and Cortazzi (1993). It is Berger's (1997) work that provides the essential features to look out for in the narrative analysis of a video tape. These include allegorical statements, metaphors, setting, tone, plot and theme. In addition, he applies Vladmir Propp's morphological approach, by identifying "kernels and satellites" as well as making a paradigmatic analysis which identifies paired opposition. (p.181).

Similar to what Raid and Johnson (1991) did in their study, Kaid's (1986) conceptualization of video style, identified the characteristics of the verbal and non-verbal video production of the political advertisement spots. She also does a categorization that identified video messages based on image or issue emphasis, policy pronouncements, positive versus negative advertisements, as well as the types of appeals commonly used in campaign commercials. The types of appeal identified include logical, emotional, ethical, and fear appeals. (Tak and Kaid, 1997, p. 8)

Comparative political communication across cultures.

Swanson (1991) referred to how problematic cross-cultural research is especially with regard to selecting a suitable theoretical approach to the study. This is because of the abstraction that often results when institutions are being examined away from their specific social and cultural contexts. The resultant distortion of meaning that arises in the course of the study often devalues vital information. (p 13). Blumler and Gurevitch (1990) contend that there is no settled view of what comparative studies should be concerned with. Neither are there alternative options for research which scholars of diverse interest and philosophic persuasions may agree on.

Roper (1996) conducted a comparative study on the cross-cultural analysis of the content of televised political advertisements in the United States and Italy. In her work, she content analyzed 90 American and 41 Italian television spots, and coded the format, strategies and use of negative attacks in the two cultures. In addition to this, she identified various styles used to convey campaign messages. These include verbal and non-verbal appeals and the production components each candidate adopted. The "transplanting" of uniquely American political communication phenomenon to another cultural setting was identified. (DAI 57/09). This trend may have gained currency in the eighties.

In her conclusion, American television spots were identified for employing more negative advertising campaign styles than their Italian counterparts. Also, Americans used more logical and fear appeals while the Italian spots were more emotional. Other methods that she identified included cinema verite style of production, music and dress codes. These methods distinguished the advertisement spots of individual politicians.

Semetko et al (1991) combined content analysis with newsroom observation in their comparative study of agenda setting role of the media. They believed that mere arithmetic calculation of advertising messages required by content analysis as a research method is unsatisfactory. They found that mass media's orientation, degree of professionalism, variation in media competition served as key factors in agenda setting roles in American and British elections. The researchers compared the roles of television journalists in British Broadcasting Corporation (BBC) and National Broadcasting Corporation (NBC), and the formation of television and the press agendas.

Their results showed that agenda setting needed to be seen as a "dynamic, not a settled procedure," (p.177) and it would be different in all countries based on political and media systems. Agenda is not solely determined by the media but by other factors like the strength of the political party system, public service versus commercial media systems, difference in level of competition in media for audiences, degree of professionalization of campaign and cultural differences.

In any study which aspires to compare political communication patterns across cultures, a close examination of differences in institutions such as the media and political set-up is necessary. This is what was done by Holtz-Bacha, Kaid and Johnston (1992) in a comparative study of United States, German and French political spots. Eighty-one campaign commercials (37 for Bush and 44 for Dukakis), 10 each for Mitterrand and Jacques Chirac, and 38 two-and-a-half-minute long political broadcasts from Germany were content analyzed. The results showed significant differences in features such as format, focus of advertisements and types of appeals. As expected, these differences were found to be a result of differences in media and political systems.

In another comparative study Tak (1993) compared of political advertisements in Korea and the United States. His was an elaborate analysis in which he not only used televised political ads but also print ads in both countries. As expected, Tak (1993) was able to re-affirm the fact that uncertainty avoidance, and non-verbal expressions were important cultural parameters that serve as determinants in the different cultural orientations in both countries. Also, that the ads used by the candidates were conspicuous indications of the different values between the two countries. (DAI-A 54/11).

In a collection of detailed study on comparative political communication, Swanson (1991), in a chapter, provides a theoretical dimension of campaign studies in the United States and France. Smith (1991) focuses on party platforms in America and France and used narrative analysis to identify narrative elements which include characters, values, and plots. Cortazzi (1993), Berger (1997), and Reissman (1993) in their various studies linked individual's life experiences, story-telling and meaning creation with culture. The aspect of meaning is crucial as Williamson showed by (1993) identifying two levels of meaning, the overt and the latent, in political advertisement. (p.12).

Mathes and Semetko (1991), in a comparative study, also provide a general assessment with emphasis on the role of television in election campaigns in developed countries. They emphasize that the differences in the information environment in these countries have a significant impact upon political communication. Making reference to the British Broadcasting Corporation (BBC), which arranges special programming to cater to the needs of political parties during campaigns, the authors implied that the role of the Parliament in BBC finances tend to make it less critical of politicians. The television networks in the Unites States where the main concern is ratings. (p. 140).

The trend of ideological shift is not an entirely new phenomenon. In a study by Haiman (1991) in which media messages of the 1988 French and American presidential elections were compared, the researcher observed that the two candidates' messages veered a little to the center of ideological spectrum. The candidates held on to their traditional loyalists as well as gain new converts at the center of the ideological spectrum.

Johnston's (1991) content analysis looked at communication strategies employed by George Bush and Francois Mitterrand. Johnston coded his data into categories made up of trustworthiness of the candidates, their competency, verbal and non-verbal styles, setting, issues and appeals as well as production styles. Of significance was the fact that the author compared 30-second spots in America with political broadcasts in France, similar to what this study intends to do with Britain and America's campaign messages. He found that the campaigns were issue-based rather than just dwelling on inconsequential matters.

In a similar study using narrative analysis, Smith (1991) compares media systems differences between France and America. He also uses the narrative approach to study the parties' platforms by breaking them into components namely, characters, values and plots. Smith argues for a comparative study that seeks to establish "equivalencies" not just "identical measures." (p. 73). Smith identified heroes, villains and fools in the stories as well as continuity, security, opportunity, and prosperity, among other issues.

Using semiological approach, Quere (1991) looked at campaign posters and related the whole process to the underlying categories of narrative syntax. Posters are crucial in political advertising campaigns and have very compelling effect on the overall campaign discourses (p.86). "It gathers and sums up what is to be found elsewhere in expanded form." (p.86).

Quere put meanings to the postures of the candidates in the posters and matched them with their key statements. Categories on which candidates were compared included modal structures, actantial roles, prominent values, syntagmatic units and actorial types. (p. 95). Quere reasoned that the poster became vital especially considering its role in binding together the three key actors in the whole political play namely, the candidate, his/her public image, and the electorate, upon all of whom successful communication depended. (p. 86).

In essence, posters serve to convey a set image to the public, enable the candidate spruce up his image and sell himself to the people. Candidate's pictures, either in posters or on television, represent the person but also carry expressions, pose, gait or demeanor that are of obvious semantic significance. (p. 88). What the candidate wears, either formal or casual, may connote relaxation versus rigor, casualness versus formality, proximity versus distance. (p. 88). There is also an analysis of "plastic and iconic aspects of the figurative manifestation." (p. 89). These include type size, and color, making posters owe much of their meaning to "positional value". (p. 90)

Advertising effect/impact

Marsh (1996) did a structural analysis and comparison of issue content in the televised political ads in the 1992 U.S. elections. The quantitative study measured issue valence using Q-sort, Q-methodology and Q-analysis to describe the structure of issue content in the selected ads.

This approach failed to reach the deep recesses of the ads from which different levels of meaning can be retrieved. It should be noted that it is defective to assume that by merely counting and correlating usage of some expression in political ads, a scholarly conclusion can be made to justify associating messages, as similar or not. Marsh, (1996) looked at how exposure to television political advertisements affected candidate image and vote likelihood ratings.

Results showed that positive spots resulted in positive image rating and negative spots meant more negative image rating. He also found that positive image rating was linked to higher vote likelihood rating more than positive issue spot. In other words, image rating counted more for positive voter perception than did positive issue commercials. This may be the reason why candidates now place more emphasis on image rather than issues.

Fairclough (1995) is quick to point out while explaining his two different but complementary forms of analysis, "linguistic and intertextual", that one cannot properly analyze content without simultaneously analyzing form and vice versa. (p.188). His summation is that "intertextual analysis mediates the connection between language and social context and facilitates more satisfactory bridging of the gap between text and contexts." (p. 189).

Kaid and Holtz-Bacha (1991, 1993) showed, in their comparative advertising effects' studies, that exposure to television broadcasts did affect images of French Prime Ministerial candidates as well as German Chancellor candidates. They explored the advertising content, style and effect through a combination of research designs that included content analysis and experimental studies over the period 1988 to 1992. Spots from United States, France, Britain, Germany, Italy and Israel were used. They followed the categorical grouping style used by Johnston (1991) and analyzed the spots under two broad categories, verbal and non-verbal messages.

The verbal group comprised of image versus issue content. The other group of verbal category includes the types of appeals used, namely emotional, logical, ethical, negative or positive appeals. The non-verbal group included the setting, narrator, use of non-verbal cues, and cinema verite production style. Although only data from four countries were used, pre and post-test design was applied to measure subjects' attitudes to candidates and their parties after exposure to some spots. They were post-tested for reaction after exposure and found that most of the advertisements were issue-centered while less emphasis was placed on parties. Also, identifiable familiar strategies were often used by challenger and incumbent candidates across cultures.

In a similar study Holtz-Bacha and Kaid (1994) conducted another research on television spots used in German elections by coding the spots into categories which included documentary, issue presentation, appeals, testimonial and production format. They found that political spots helped in shaping voter evaluation of candidates. (p.67). Johnston and Gerstle's (1995) study also found a similar effect of political spots on presidential candidates in France. Using content analysis, political broadcasts and clips of Francois Mitterrand and Jacques Chirac were compared in this study.

The issue of humor in political spots was addressed by Voight (1997). Using Kenneth Burke's comic frame of acceptance in a political context, he outlined the comic media styles. He explored the relationship between content and presentational elements in radio and television advertisements. The results were that humor is vital and effective in any study of comparative political spots. He argued in favor of humor in political advertising noting that it does not constitute a negative effect. He also raised questions that categorizing humor in political advertising as "negative campaign tactics" is defective. (DAI-A 57/09 p.3749, March 1997).

Many scholars used the agenda setting approach to determine the impact of political advertising on either, the news media, the electorate or even the politicians. McCombs (1979) determined that there was a causal relationship between media reports and the issues perceived as important by the electorate. In other words, voters learned from media reports to make voting decisions. McCombs and Shaw (1972) established that the media influenced how people perceived what was of importance in a campaign.

Brosius and Kepplinger (1992), in a comparative content analysis, sought to determine how agenda setting influenced behavior. They used the 1986 German Parliamentary election in this study and determined that not only does media agenda go beyond affecting the salience of issues but also that the salience will affect other political perceptions and attitudes.

Kaid (1991) pointed to a convergence of opinion on the Americanization of campaign styles in Europe, especially in France as the reason for her study. She studied the effects of television broadcast on subjects' perception of candidates. Using pre-test and post-test research design, questionnaire and video viewing, reactions of subjects chosen from the United States and France were compared on their perceptions of presidential candidates in the two countries. Results showed "remarkably similar television-induced perceptions of presidential candidates." (p. 257). The study found that there were strong correlations between emotions evoked by television broadcasts and candidate image perceptions in both countries.

Americanization or globalization of political communication styles

The issue of whether other countries of the world are following America's political campaign styles has generated a lot of attention in political communication literature. An examination of a collection of cross-country research work on political communication indicates the glaring differences in media systems across the world. Yet, according to Mancini and Swanson (1996), it appears that the patterns of political communication changes seem to converge, especially around those styles often identified to be American. They referred to the alluring "mythology of the great power of United States' elections campaign practices." (p.5).

Valuable contributions have been made by a number of researchers including Day, 1982; Mancini and Swanson 1994; Blumler, 1991; and Negrine, 1996. Some of these authors believe that the influence of America's overall political culture indeed goes beyond mere campaign styles. Are we then witnessing a trend whereby political communication in all other parts of the world will be dictated by styles imported from America?

Kaid, Gerstle and Sanders (1991) describe Americanized political system as the use of media techniques which tend to heighten candidate image instead of party loyalties. (p.1). Day's (1982) study identified British importation of techniques of commercial marketing from America which are believed to have started around 1970.

Day claimed that this application of American political campaign experiences on Britain was pioneered by the Conservative Party (p.5). Some of the features of this importation included sharp and pungent messages, or what he called "capsulization" of messages (p.8).

However, Scammell et al. (1995) claimed that American techniques were imported to Britain way back in the 60's when Harold Wilson studied John Kennedy's television manners. (p. 41). They noted that the feeling in Britain regarding this influence was that British politics was being "coarsened, even corrupted" by the importation of American techniques. (p.21). Americanization, to these authors, is the "elevation of personality, glitz, glamour, emotional, often negative appeals" in campaigns. (p. 21).

With specific reference to the last General elections in Britain, Rosenbaum, in *U.S. News and World Report*, observed that, "'Americanization' [of British] politics is clearly occurring. You might call it the trivialization, with politicians speaking in shorter and shorter sound bites." Mancini and Swanson (1996) identified the features of Americanized political campaigning as "personalization of politics, scientification of politics and styles, detachment of citizens from the parties, and autonomous structures of communication." (pp. 5-6).

That democracies all over the world are copying America's political campaign styles is not entirely a new phenomenon. Indeed, it can be said that America has been setting the pace in many respects, with profound copycat effects on the rest of the world. Jamieson (1996) claimed that television messages are the offshoot of songs, banners, torches used hundreds of years ago. America has brought "a modern professional edge to the once old-fashioned gentlemanly world of British politics." *U.S. News and World Report*, (May 5, 1997).

However, Pfetsch and Schmitt-Beck (1993) say that the American political communication is fraught with pure marketing techniques, otherwise labeled "New

Politics." (p. 6). This is comparable to the techniques marketers use to push products into the market and the consciousness of the consumers. In essence, this could be referred to as the commodification of political communication.

It is Maarek (1995) who differentiates political communication from political marketing. Political communication, he noted, is a mere general term used to refer to how political communicators "'communicated' with their publics," while political marketing is a recent development involving a "strategy of design, rationalization and conveyance of modern political communication which often include entire marketing process, from preliminary market study to testing and targeting." (p. 28).

Kaid and Holtz-Bacha (1995) identified characteristics of American type political communication as "the predominance of images instead of issues, their personalization of politics, and the professionalization of political actors in the development of media strategies." (pp. 8-9). Scammell (1998) described the conversion of voters into consumers with the increasing professionalization of communication, when political campaigns designed for media overshadow traditional forms of voter mobilization, and "image" politics becomes the norm.

Scammell (1998) also reasoned that the more professional America's political styles become, the more exportable they will be. (p.252). Also, he insisted that globalization does not translate to Americanization especially since it was found that the British Conservative party assisted George Bush in the 1992 presidential elections.

Besides, the Tories contracted Saatchi and Saatchi, originally a British advertising agency for their campaigns just as did the Russian government, evidently catching the flu of modern-day political communication strategies. To Scammell, however, Americanization of political campaign strategies may just well be a contested terminology, especially because those who use the term based on just surface similarities, obscure salient national differences, variations and adaptations.

This is one of the factors why such a study as this one will be able to find out how American and British political communication styles were similar or different in the last elections held in both countries.

Chapter III

Theoretical Framework

Studies that employ a critical approach are capable of enhancing our understanding of the world around us, the people and their beliefs, and indeed the whole society. Essentially, historical-cultural analysis does all or some of the following: a comparative analysis of likeness and difference, study of trends, their occurrences and an exploration of how the depth of issues enable us to draw logical conclusions.

Critical studies incorporate careful organization, systematic and thorough description, analysis, and interpretation in explaining the relationships among symbols.(Berg, Wenner and Gronbeck, 1998, p.29). More popular in England and parts of Europe, critical studies research veered away from its traditional foundations to a new area called British Cultural Studies in the eighties. Research study conducted by the Glasgow Media Group in 1981 examined the issue of racism in news discourse in the British media.

Various studies were conducted by scholars like Stuart Hall, and Raymond Williams but Fiske (1978 and 1987) opened new vistas in critical studies research. He describes television as "provokers of meaning and pleasure" rather than "makers of meanings". (p.29). In a nutshell, criticism could be referred to as "informed talk about matters of importance." (p. 29).

Each critical approach ought to be "multi-dimensional" (p.45) as this ensures that all critics do "not end up with same things." (p.45). To avoid the pitfalls encountered by the blind men in the famous blind men fable, critical analysis needs

59

to be conscious of the trap of partiality. No matter how thoroughly conducted, critical studies still suffer from the inadequacy of incompleteness.

Critical analysts could be likened to the fabled blind men that happened upon an elephant, with each one holding on to the part of the huge animal's body they could touch. The one that held on to the head had a different view of the elephant from the one who held the trunk, the leg or the tail. Each told his story of the elephant from the perspective based on what part of the elephant he had touched.

Critical tradition began with literary criticism and structuralist linguistics, but it encompasses a range of perspectives including psychoanalysis, feminism and ideological analysis. Some of these techniques are employed in the analysis of the text in this study.

Method of Analysis

Qualitative research methodology remains a very contentious area of research in mass communication. Not only are the researchers within the behavioral school believe that it is defective, it is sometimes accused of being rather too subjective. The fact that many of the adherents of the qualitative research approach seem to shy away from providing succinct definition of that research approach seems to make things more difficult.(Potter, 1996).

Definitions of the qualitative research methodology are as many as they are diversified in scope. Strauss and Corbins (1990), in their simple and direct definition, state that, "It is any kind of research that produces findings that are not arrived at by means of statistical procedures or other means of quantification." (p.17). Some of the steps to arriving at such findings include finding a topic, formulating research questions, gathering the evidence, interpreting the evidence and telling the researcher's story. (Pauly, 1991).

The diversified nature of qualitative research methodology is contained in Smith's (1987) definition which describes it as "richly variegated and its theories of method diverse to the point of disorderliness." (p.173). Despite the rather "richly variegated" nature of this research methodology, its holistic advance in the examination of issues in an organic manner, cannot be over-emphasized. Bogdan and Taylor (1975) note that qualitative research removes itself from the, disjointed and disorganized approach, common with the quantitative methodology.

In other words, qualitative research explores issues which ordinarily quantitative studies may be ineffective at doing. When the issue to be analyzed is human communication, the concern is often that the application of a quantitative methodology will fail to capture the rich complexity involved. When a research tool fails to untangle the complexity in human communication, such a tool only diminishes the rich experience inherent in human expression. Beyond mere words expressed verbally, human communication is embedded in codes that translate cultural representations, moods, symbols, emotions and state of mind.

To assume that qualitative research does not employ any form of quantification or statistical analysis may be faulty. Sometimes, quantitative methods made up of statistical findings, are often incorporated into qualitative research in combination with qualitative research tools. The only difference is that such an approach goes beyond what quantitative research does. This is by reaching into the inner meanings into those statistical figures in a holistic fashion.

Turner (1990) refers to how qualitative research has crossed disciplinary barriers by shaping our knowledge of situations. This helps us unravel the complexity inherent in cultural issues. Carey's (1989) study is emphatic as he refers to qualitative research as that study that provides us with a clearer and reflexive relationship of scholarship to society.

Whereas quantitative research applies the "transmission" route to communication, qualitative researchers attempt to unravel the shared systems of meaning. And unlike quantitative research that arrogates cause-effect perspective to communication, which is an aspect of human behavior, qualitative researchers focus on "symbolic dramas by which groups articulate and integrate those demographic identities." (Pauly, 1991 p.6).

Research techniques

For this study, the researcher chose not to adopt a single research method in the analysis of political campaign messages, since the study cut across two countries. This is because choosing a single approach will not allow the researcher to bring forth all the levels of meaning embedded in the political messages.

Political advertising may pose as a "treacherous arena..." where appearances and meanings are constructed and destroyed. (Biocca, 1991, p.5). To unpack the meaning, we must, therefore, understand not only the cognitive process of reception but the social construction, circulation and transformation of the codes the (message) advertisements contain. (p.6).

The cross-cultural and cross-national nature of this research work calls for a few qualitative research methods to capture the comparative scope of the research objective. Kaid, Gerstle and Sanders (1991) recommend a combination of methods that incorporate content analysis and observation to complement each other especially in a cross-national communication system comparison. (p.183).

In a similar observation, Van Dijk (1988) submits that in analyzing media discourses, emphasis should be on the language structures at various levels of description (p.2). This is why this study employed the use of some research methods that included semiotics, ideological, discourse and narrative analyses for examining the political messages. Morreale's (1993) textual frame analysis of late President

Reagan's speech was used as a model to reach balanced conclusions and answer the research question posed on production styles of the candidates.

Some authors in the area of political communication like Blumler and Gurevitch (1975) contend that

> there is neither a settled view of what (comparative) studies should be concerned with, nor even a firmly crystallized set of alternative options for research between which scholars of diverse philosophic persuasions could choose. (p. 105).

To add credence to this view, editors of *Political Communication Yearbook* agreed that,

> the varied experiences brought into the study area... are so varied and pluralist in outlook and approach,... it is a mistake to adhere slavishly to any set format in shaping the content. (Morreale, 1993, p.vii).

There is some latitude in this approach in the search for complete meanings of messages.

Adhering to the notion that human communication is rendered meaningless when taken out of context, the study took care to knit the parts into a whole to create meaning. This was done by examining the settings and the individuals within them in a holistic fashion. This ensured that the subject of the study was not transformed into an isolated variable or a hypothesis. This put the study outside the realm of quantitative approach which espouses "reductionistic number crunching." (Potter, 1996, p. 10).

A holistic approach to analysis of campaign commercials becomes necessary considering that all political commercials are in the form of packaged information framed in discursive or narrative structures. They are also made up of "sets of codes, discourses and semantic frames." (Biocca, 1991, p.34). Therefore, this study employed the some of the common techniques used by critical studies" scholars to analyze the research data. These include narrative, semiological, and ideological analyses.

Database and Research Materials

Primary research materials for this study consisted of video tapes of campaign messages of President Bill Clinton and those of Prime Minister Tony Blair. These were collected from the Democratic National Committee (DNC) of America and the Labour Party of Britain. Four campaign video tapes, two from each country, contained short campaign messages and full- length party convention speeches by the two candidates. Whereas the two Clinton tapes contained altogether 35 thirty-second commercials, the Blair tapes contained seven five-to-ten minute Party Election Broadcasts (PEB). Running time for all the tapes was approximately 180 minutes.

The Clinton tapes were broadcast on television networks shortly before the 1996 presidential elections. Unlike the Blair tapes that aired simultaneously on all television channels in Britain, those of Bill Clinton ran separately all over the country. Emphasis in terms of air-time was on those states with more electoral votes.

The more than an hour-long party convention speech of President Clinton was delivered on August 29, 1996 in Chicago following days of train journey from Washington via the heartland of America. It was the speech that followed soon after he won the Democratic Party's nomination along with Vice President Al Gore. The party conference speech of the Labour party took place in London. The running time for the Labour Party tapes was about one hour thirty minutes.

The choice of television video tapes as the only medium of communication to be analyzed stems from the ubiquitous nature of television especially its potency in influencing its audiences. (Smith and Nimmo, 1991). American political communication has experienced significant transformation from the era when politicians, like Harry Truman in 1948, traversed thousands of miles to get their political messages across to the audiences to the current "telepolitical age."

Television began to dominate political communication in the United States from around 1952 changing not just America's political culture but indeed that of all developed countries of the world. (Morreale, p.1). Television is said to have offered producers of campaign discourse some "Svengalian powers" that print and radio lacked. In addition, television is said to reinforce "reality in ways that heighten the powers of the visceral appeal." (Jamieson, 1992, pp. 9-10).

The audience for Party Election Broadcasts in 1992 British election was estimated at about 13 million, by every means a low figure. It was not until around 1979 when major parties started to inject life into their Party Election Broadcasts turning it away from the format of the "gray suited politician speaking woodenly to a camera." (Kaid, and Holtz Bacha, 1995, p.20). A new genre of political communication seems to have emerged in the last fifteen years in not only Britain but the rest of Europe which also raises the question if a global political communication pattern may be emerging.

The following chapter examines the themes and social values contained in the texts under analysis. The purpose here was to identify the salient points contained in the tapes. This helped in pinpointing how the two leaders employed various approaches to get their messages across and how meanings were packaged in the messages.

Chapter IV

Textual Analysis of Themes and Values

Bill Clinton: "The bridge to the 21st century"

The following paragraphs serve the purpose of exploring the surface level of the messages. This is by identifying the core values and themes contained in the texts. Following this effort is the analysis of the underlying meanings contained in the texts.

The major themes and values in the campaign messages were identified by their recurrence in the sentences and the emphasis placed on them. According to Stillar (1998), "thematic information in messages is structured in terms of the ordering and position of elements in a sentence." (p. 46). Sometimes, such themes are also determined by their positions within the sentence structures. It is the combination of the thematic structure of a message and the cohesive devices applied in form of style that not only distinguishes one speaker from the other, but also contributes to the "texture of the text." (p 46).

Protecting the elderly (Medicare and Medicaid)

This was a dominant campaign issue which Clinton hinged his campaign upon. He attempted to position his candidacy as the one that had the interests of the elderly and vulnerable senior citizens at heart. In doing this, it was quite easy to link the Republican Party presidential candidate, Bob Dole and House Speaker Newt Gingrich, as hardened and unrepentant hard-liners who will stop at nothing to sacrifice the interests of the elderly just to balance the budget. Clinton paraded himself as standing up for the elderly by his veto of the bill which called for huge reduction in Medicaid and Medicare to balance the budget.

This theme resonated in the rhetoric and served the purpose of playing to the gallery, portraying the Grand Old Party (GOP) as anti-senior citizens. Bob Dole and Newt Gingrich, thus appeared as the demons who wanted the Medicaid protection of the elderly to "wither in the vine," especially in all campaign commercials that had themes around Medicare and Medicaid. (See Appendix A, xviii).

One other recurrent theme was that of reforming welfare and moving state-dependent families to jobs. Entwined with the theme of welfare reform are the issues of creation of more jobs, and the enhancement of family values. The themes were echoed more by testimonials provided by "ordinary citizens" who had been on the government dole but moved to get a job following the Clinton formula of more jobs for all. (Appendix A, xxviii).

The theme of crime and the public dominated the campaign commercials, especially with the emotional impact that the images of fallen policemen conveyed in the commercials. The proposal of hiring 100,000 more policemen to keep the American people safe from criminals is heavily relied upon to send the message that the Democrats were safety conscious.

Traditionally, focus on crime reduction had been a Republican issue. Bill Clinton, through his own proposal of providing assistance to local communities for hiring additional policemen cleverly preempted this important Republican issue.

Clinton centered the shift in his ideological stance on attracting "natural Democrats" who had voted earlier for the Republicans back into the fold. This was a lesson he learned from 1992 following his defeat of the Republican president George Bush. Before then, the Republicans had been in the presidency for 12 years. (Brown, 1997, p. 481). He did this by appealing to the concerns of the middle class, jettisoning the age-old Democrat's image associated with high taxes, big spending and was linked to minority interests. (p. 481). Issues of concern to the middle class included fighting crime, reducing unemployment, lowering taxes and providing support for education.

In its 1996 Party Platform, the Democratic Party shed its previous identity and instead aligned itself with the Republican rhetoric. Some of the lines included, "Today's Democratic Party is determined to renew America's most basic bargain: Opportunity to every American, and responsibility from every American." (*Democratic Platform*, August 27, 1996, p. 1). The cardinal objectives were, Opportunity, Responsibility, and Community. The Democratic Party offered the American people the following: The end of big government, encouraging people to get off welfare, safe neighborhoods and quality education. The Democrats also promised to fulfill their duties to the senior citizens, lower taxes, provide cleaner environment and provide more jobs. All of these are traditional Republican messages.

In line with this, there were regular references to the popular Brady Bill, signed into law by Clinton, which prescribes a mandatory waiting period to check the background of hand-gun purchases. The shots on hand-gun controls were the most emotional, in which fear and anxiety appeals were used to the fullest. Shots of officers killed in the line of duty or their formal burial ceremonies were delivered in solemn images and tone. (See Appendix A, xii, xiv).

The Democrats appealed to working parents with children in college by emphasizing the need for quality and affordable education for all. In the Convention speech delivered in Chicago, Clinton promised the electorate tax deductible savings for higher education for working families. A key issue that dominated the campaign commercials under study and appealed mostly to middle class Americans who are burdened by the rising costs of college education. A promise of wiring all schools to the Internet and ensuring that all five-year olds are able to read and write formed the cornerstones of the theme of education.

Closely linked to this was the very sensitive issue of escalating incidence of cigarette smoking and drug use by school-age children. Buoyed by the active contribution of Vice President Al Gore, the theme of eradicating drug use in schools resonated all through the campaign video tapes analyzed.

Padded with emotional narratives, the theme of war on drugs amplified by the story of how Clinton's brother was rescued from the throes of destruction when he fought back drug addiction. The powerful effect of this narrative was to convey how debilitating the consequences of drug addiction can be on any family, the president's family included.

Clean environment, fresh air and pollution-free neighborhoods and cities were some of the concerns expressed in the tapes. In most of the shots analyzed the Democrat accused the opposing party of pursuing environment policies that fell short of the international requirements for a safe environment.

The importance of cleaner environment was necessitated by the growing concerns for the unpredictably inclement weather conditions that have been witnessed in parts of the country recently. These have been attributed to environmental pollution, a campaign which Clinton and vice president Al Gore in particular, hold very dear to heart. The messages emphasized cleaning the environment of toxic wastes, penalizing organizations that pursue non-efficient toxic waste disposal policies and ensuring cleaner air, water, and land for posterity. "I want to build a bridge to the 21st century with a clean and safe environment," Bill Clinton promised the electorate.

Bill Clinton tapes emphasized the issue of tax reduction for working families. Most of the commercials were geared toward refuting the tax-raising image that the opponents have identified him with. Most of the time Clinton's promise of lower tax for working families often recurred in statements and testimonials of actors who acted as ordinary folks in the commercials.

Indeed the allusion to the theme of a dying century was the cornerstone of Bill Clinton commercials. The theme of the Democratic Party Convention speech was "The bridge to the 21st century" (See Appendix A, xxix), in which the pending new millennium was alluded to as the harbinger of good things for the American people. The phrase, "bridge to the 21st century", was used in almost twenty different scenes, especially during the convention speech. Other closely associated themes were hope, the future, dream, aspirations, vision, and other futuristic references that seemed to signpost a forward-looking administration. This strategy was to neutralize Bob Dole's campaign which relied on the theme of good old days, appealing to the sense of the old glorious days.

The campaign messages depended on the new millennium agenda which the Democrats wanted the voters to be a part of. The emotion is played upon here as the refrain in the messages entreated the citizens to join hands with Clinton in building "the bridge to the 21st century."

Bill Clinton used the expression that referred to the bridge to the 21st century over twenty times in the nearly 120-minute Convention speech. Other closely associated themes were hope for the people, the American dream, individual aspirations and how they can be met, vision and the future.

These futuristic references that seemed to sign-post a forward-looking image for the Democrats served as a careful strategy to effectively energize the voters and also neutralize the "good old days' appeal of Bob Dole which alluded to the better yesterdays. The bridge metaphor thus served a multiplicity of purposes. It was not just to serve as a passage to the future, as opposed to using it as a route to the past it was to ensure a forward-looking attitude to the good life we all have now.

The campaign messages relied upon the new millennium agenda of Bill Clinton which he wanted the voters to be a part of. The reference to the twenty-first century as the desired destination is also not lost on us. It refers to time. It depicts progression, continuity, hinting at a subtle air of urgency in accomplishing all that is required to have better days ahead.

The apt metaphor of the bridge is not to be missed here as the futuristic objective of that call is as important as the invaluable role a bridge can play in a racially diverse society. The call serves the dual purpose of a bridge to the future as well as a bridge to interracial harmony among the many ethnically diverse groups of American society.

President Clinton drew on the well-accepted status of the United States as the superpower and emphasized the theme of global peace, security and cooperation to deal with international terrorism. Invoking the "American spirit" to convey his message of international peace and security, he promised to fight terrorism as if he would be engaged in a physical war, "with a three-pronged strategy." He used the fear appeal to drive home his point; "terrorists are as big a threat to our future, perhaps bigger than organized crime." This sublime threat connotes the need for action to rid the world of trouble makers. And that can be achieved if people vote the Democrats into power.

The goal of a balanced budget and prosperity for all was also dominant in the themes identified. Indeed the issue of budget deficit and the difference in proposed solution between the Democrats and Republicans led to the shutdown of government shortly before the elections. Bill Clinton used the closure to drive home his point that he would do anything to prevent harsh budgetary cuts on essential programs like Medicare and Medicaid, popular among majority of Americans. The recurrence of this theme in Clinton's campaign served to further demonize the Republican duo of Bob Dole and Newt Gingrich. Without a doubt, Clinton did not spare his opponents for the government shut down that his administration was confronted with. He got much better mileage out of the incident than did his opponents.

New Labor: Tony Blair's Campaign themes

The most common theme in the campaign messages of Tony Blair was that of a political rebirth. A rebirth for the Labour Party and a rebirth for the British people who were being promised better times by the newly refurbished Labour Party.

The Party slogan, "New Labour", was aptly and effectively exploited in the campaign messages. The newness of the party was backed up by new themes of regeneration, inclusiveness and a brighter future ahead. The simple message was built around Tony Blair's message in which he said, "our case is simple; that Britain can and must be better... The vision is one of national renewal, a country with drive, purpose and energy." (Blair, 1997, pp. 2-3).

The significance of the newness was evident in the come-back posture and business-like approach of the Labour Party which was poised to wrest power from the Tory Party that had been in power for 18 years. This was reinforced by the shedding of those vestiges of radicalism that stigmatized the Labour Party as a radical, high taxation party.

The removal of Clause Four heralded a rebirth for the Labor Party. Clause Four of the Labor Party constitution was one of the key articles that gave the party its socialist image, considered good or bad, depending on one's ideological leanings. Tossing away this clause, the age-long encumbrance to gaining power, represented a re-birth for the party just as much as the take-over from the Tories would translate into a political re-birth for Britain.

Another key issue was that of education. Tony Blair's acclaimed first three priorities, as told in the commercials, were "education, education, education"! (Labor

Party Election Broadcast, 1997). The challenge of reducing class size by half and ensuring that the children are able to attend school without hindrance was daunting to say the least.

As did Bill Clinton, Blair also emphasized the need for reducing crime rate by hiring more law enforcement officers. One of the key messages of Blair's campaign was epitomized in the slogan: "Tough on crimes, tough on the causes of crimes". The crime prevention agenda included reducing bureaucracy within the law enforcement offices, instituting a ban on the use of handguns, and paying more prompt attention to the victims of crimes.

In reference to the 18-year rule of the Tories in Britain, Blair's campaign theme touched on the issue of renovating the medical system in Britain, the National Health Service (NHS). Passionate messages revolved around reducing waiting lists in hospitals especially for cancer surgery, higher quality treatment for patients, cutting waste in the NHS, spending and encouraging good health for the British people.

The Tony Blair campaign tapes enunciated the values of getting 250,000 Britons off welfare and promised them new jobs. Another issue was that of introducing tax cuts for employers that created new jobs. The value of employment is amplified by other incentives like job training and after-school care for single parents who plan to get a job.

The Labor Party moved away from its traditional role of state welfare economy to that of promoting personal prosperity for all, reduction of taxes, and mortgage rates, promotion of investment and savings and avoiding budget deficits. The baggage of Clause Four was shed as the hope for taking power became brighter.

The promotion of family values was also one of the key themes that cut across the campaign messages of Tony Blair. This was crucial to the middle-class income group that the Labor Party hoped to appeal to. It was promised in the messages that homelessness, an eye-sore of the British society, would be tackled.

One other theme emphasized the need for installing rectitude in the society by encouraging citizens to "get more out of life." Blair promised to set up a citizen's service for a new millennium. The focus will be improving the quality of social life for the citizens so they can optimally realize their potential. This will be done through the promotion of sports, arts and culture, and clean environment.

Labour also promised accountability in public offices, devolution of power in Scotland and Wales, elected Mayors for London and other cities and the pursuit of complete peace in Northern Ireland. This promise was made as a way to assuage the citizens that make up the United Kingdom who have long sought after some form of autonomy from the British government. These include Northern Ireland, Scotland and Wales.

The role of Britain in Europe and the world was critical in the campaign. The opposing Conservative Party faced disintegration essentially because of European Union dissenters in the party ranks who were opposed to Britain's policy on Europe. John Redwood Secretary for Wales in the Tory government was one of the dissenters. The contention was that Britain should take a leading role rather than be a follower in Europe. It appeared that the Tory government had not forcefully pursued British interests in Europe. It was thus used as a critical factor in the campaign messages of the Labour Party.

Tony Blair talked about ensuring a new age where hope is kept alive. "There is no future for Britain as a low-wage, low-skill, low-technology economy," he reasoned. He, therefore, promised a stable economy, long term investments and low taxes. To back this up, he actually promised that the Labour Party would not raise taxes at all on low-income workers for the entire period of his first term. This was a smart scheme that soon became a good campaign issue in the year 2002.

There will be support for the industry and wholesome assistance for the manufacturing sector, the Labour Party promised. Also, support services will be provided for science and engineering, research and development as well as tax incentives to aid industry production.

Chapter V
Critical Analysis of Texts

Bill Clinton

The analysis of the text was done by adopting Berg, Wenner and Gronbeck's (1998) method of categorization of televisual communication. In the first category grouped under verbal codes/linguistic units, the texts were analyzed using sub-categories such as attitudinal language, valuative language, metaphorical language and ideological language. In these categories, semiotics, structuralist as well as discourse analysis were used to decipher meanings in the video tapes.

Each commercial, with running time of 30 seconds and over was reduced to shots for ease of analysis. The resultant units or frames of reference, were then examined for codes and signs that conveyed meanings. References are made to the texts for examples that fit into any of the categories being examined.

For Bill Clinton sixty 30-second commercials were analyzed with each commercial broken down to between ten and fifteen shots. A shot is a "continuous take of the camera with no break in time." (Porter, 1983, p. 70). The multiple shots, comprising hundreds of images, enabled the communication of messages, symbols and actions that conveyed effective meanings.

At the next level, especially with the longer campaign speeches which ran for between five and one hundred and twenty minutes, scenes were categorized for ease of analysis. Scenes refer to two or more continuous shots in which actions take longer and more images are recorded. Due to the high number of shots identified, each shot

77

was not isolated for analysis but rather, were analyzed based on the themes they contained.

Verbal Codes: Linguistic units

Shots were separated by determining how people in the texts were identified or named. (p.96). The key actors in the shots, except individuals used for testimonials were Bill Clinton, Bob Dole his opponent, and Newt Gingrich, the House Speaker. In all the shots analyzed in which any of these actors were referred to, all except Bill Clinton were referred to using only their last names.

For example, one of the statements in the commercial said:

> Bob Dole and Newt Gingrich tried to cut vaccines for children... Also on Medicare and Medicaid, the ad ran, Dole and Gingrich tried to slash Medicare...Dole even voted to make it easier for corporations to raid pensions...

Whereas all references to Bill Clinton had his title of president, such honor was not extended to Senator Bob Dole and Speaker Newt Gingrich. This conveyed a presidential air for Mr. Clinton while the titles of the opponents were conspicuously omitted. It was used to create a bridge of distinction between Bill Clinton and his opponents without titles.

Attitudinal language category sought to establish what and how words were used to express positive or negative judgments about the principal actors. It was observed that any reference to the opponents in the Bill Clinton tapes, Bob Dole and Newt Gingrich, were portrayed in the negative light. When the titles of the opponents were not mentioned, it became easier to lash out at them.

Bob Dole and Newt Gingrich were labeled as unyielding, uncooperative and unfriendly in their opposition to programs that would benefit the senior citizens and children. The message suggested that the Medicaid and education would have suffered if Bill Clinton had allowed the budget cuts they proposed to pass.

References to those close to Bob Dole were equally uncomplimentary. Bob Dole was accused of desperate attacks and in the shot, was referred to as "The senator most responsible for blocking any serious campaign finance reform." Bob Dole was said to be "wrong in the past, wrong for our future." Also that his "old ways don't work," playing the age card here, and that "the new way" is what will meet our challenges, and protect our values.

In "Dole votes No", (Appendix A, xii) Clinton message accused Dole of voting "No" to the proposal to "ban assault weapons, provide family leave, achieve balanced budget, protect Medicare..." A rhyming sound reinforced a negative image reminding the voters repeatedly, "Dole votes No". Gingrich on the other hand, was associated with "gridlock" and "shutdown."

In terms of valuative language, some of Bill Clinton's shots appealed to the moral, religious, social, psychological and aesthetic sense of the American people. Values such as compassion, care, and respect for senior citizens, love of family, respect for the rule of law and duty to self and the society were some of those coded in the shots. References to "what is right for the elderly", "our duty to our seniors", taking care of the sick and the vulnerable children," allusion to the Constitution, "our forefathers", and the flag all aroused in the viewers a sense of nationalism and duties of a welfare state.

Valuative language refers to those messages coded in moral, aesthetic and religious tone. Bill Clinton's messages embedded those values that appealed to the electorate across racial, social, economic, and perhaps political biases. Such language use laden with valuative import was common in all the shots.

In the commercial on welfare, the message said, "Families destroyed, children's dreams lost, the legacy of our present welfare system. The president's plan..." Another shot said: "There are beliefs and values that tie Americans together. In Washington these values get lost in the tug of war..." In one of the campaign shots, it was said: "As Americans, there are some things we do simply and solely because they are moral, right and good. Treating our elderly with dignity is one of these things..."

Metaphorical language

Due to the multiple usage of metaphors both at the textual and visual levels, the metaphors discussed under this section will be limited to the text alone while visual metaphors are discussed under the section on visual images.

In the shots that conveyed messages about Medicare and Medicaid cuts, an array of metaphors were used. Bill Clinton promised to "protect America." Most of the shots acclaimed Bill Clinton as the one to protect Medicare and Medicaid, the American values. In another metaphor, Newt Gingrich was quoted as saying about Medicare and Medicaid that, "Now we don't get rid of it in round one...We don't think that the right way to go through a transition. But we believe it's going to wither in the vine."

It must be mentioned that the references to cuts in Medicare and Medicaid could be said to be metaphorical in the sense that it is not possible to cut funds, you can reduce them. The use of "cut" as if applying an axe to the funds was a mere exaggeration that could pass for a metaphor.

The policy on drug abuse was featured with war metaphors. Bill Clinton said he appointed a four-star general as if it was a real battle against drug use in America. In another war metaphor, the impasse between the White House and the Congress that resulted in the close-down of government offices was called "the tug of war" in Washington. This was in "New-York Sand", one of the 30-second shots. (See Appendix A, xviii, xix, xx).

Above all, it is the underlying metaphorical language used that makes Bill Clinton's language use more effective. Metaphors are the "cognitive devices for forming and communicating conceptualizations of reality which may be in some way problematic." (Chillon and Schaffner, 1997, p.222).

The metaphor of the past and the future, a subtle play on Bob Dole's old age and his senior-citizen status, effectively conveyed the message of hope for the future rather than the despondency of yesterday. Bob Dole was said to be "wrong in the past and wrong for the future," and that "their old ways don't work."

Another good use of metaphor was the reference to the "bridge to the 21st century', the theme of Bill Clinton's convention speech. "We will build that "bridge to the 21st century' with more opportunity, more responsibility and a stronger community for all of us." (See Appendix A, xxix). The metaphor here was in making the 21st century assume the look of a destination that can be reached by car or train, being the two means of transportation that use bridge for crossing. Bridges are used for crossing and there was a futuristic tinge in the way Clinton used this to neutralize Bob Dole's call for a step back to the old glorious days. The emphasis of this metaphor pitched Clinton and Dole against each other, one forward looking, the other despondent, pessimistic and backward looking.

Ideological analysis

Ideological analysis tends to explain issues more from cultural perspective than most other approaches. Indeed, it is called the "science of ideas". (Williams, 1983). Ideological analysis of the media has been done from various perspectives depending on which school of thought the researcher comes from. Marxist approach is one of the popular ones, deriving its perspective from Marxist historians, political scientists, and economists. (Berger, 1991 p.32). Even within the Marxist perspective, various strands of thoughts have begun to emerge due to the rapidly changing nature of ideological analysis.

The huge capital outlay involved in the creation of political advertisements has made the issue of materialism as defined by Marx in *Preface to a Contribution* to the *Critique of Political Economy* relevant here. It argues that the structure of the society constitutes the real foundation on which social, legal and political superstructures are built. As a result, definite forms of social consciousness conform and correspond to these institutions. (Berger, 1991). The general character of a people's social, political and spiritual survival depends upon the production of material life.

The Marxist ideology is based on the belief that all things are shaped and determined by economic system of a society which in an indirectly subtle fashion interacts to affect how men form ideas about themselves. Such ideas go to form the basis for the arrangements within the society, about how and what institutions are formed and how they relate with each other.

Therefore, applying Marxist ideological approach to the analysis of media content enables us to assess the role played by the means of production in shaping our ideas, values, notions, concepts, and beliefs that the media help to disperse. In political advertising messages such as are being analyzed in this study, we see the process of shaping the perceptions and beliefs of the majority about candidates and their capabilities through the manipulation and control of the media by a few. Consumers of media messages tend to take for granted the contents of the media as being representative of the views of the majority.

What Classical Marxism holds is that the capitalist elite that controls the means of production, including the media industry, create and reinforce their views and opinions to a point that the proletariat, begins to assume that their views represent the natural order of things. They thus help perpetuate the process of their own oppression. (Berger, 1991)

In essence, because the means of production or the economic base determine the structure of institutions which are built upon it, Marxist base-superstructure approach assumes that those who control the means of production (base) ultimately have control over whatever is built upon it (the superstructure). Institutions and values in any society are shaped by the means of production.

Scholars like Gramsci (1971) believe in the existence of competing multiple ideologies, one of which is the dominant and the other subordinate. His study comes readily to mind especially in the analysis of campaign video tapes in this study. The competition of ideologies is not just between the ruling elite and the masses but also between and among the dominant political ideologues who are seeking top positions in government. The emerging trend of ideological shift to the center has been identified in most western democracies as well. We are told that the coercive nature of the dominant groups are now less forceful as in the past. However, this is not to underestimate the power of sublime coercion contained in advertising messages. Indeed for our generation, television serves as the predominating tool for "normalizing or naturalizing the existing social order." (Berg, Wenner and Gronbeck, 1998, p. 293).

All advertising is said to contain ideology, (O'Barr, 1994), and no commercial can be read for total meaning without employing some ideological tools. Ideological analysis can be applied into reading an advertisement by focusing on cultural undertones in the message as well as the social relationships between the people depicted in the advertisement. (Frith, 1997). Television serves to explore and exploit how economic, social and political relationships can be reinforced through messages.

There is a discernible trend that democratic institutions in most developed nations of the world are shifting from rightist conservatism and leftist pseudo-communism to the center of the ideological spectrum. The rhetoric of the politicians analyzed in the video tapes is reflective of this ideological shift. There is a struggle within the elite class, to take control of the government by subtle persuasion using political advertising appeals.

Ideological analysis is thus used in this study as a tool for identifying those traits that give rise to ideological warfare. Political advertising is one of the important mechanisms used by the elite to disseminate their messages to their audiences. Political advertisements, therefore, provide a fertile source of material for examination from an ideological perspective.

There seems to be a link between how capitalism has heightened consumption by exploiting the impulsive nature of human beings and the way politicians seek to persuade prospective voters. According to this Marxist ideological perspective, advertising "diverts people's attention from social and political concerns into narcissistic and private concerns." (Berger, 1991, p.44).

This is because the authority of the dominant elite is

> perpetuated both through overt propaganda in political rhetoric, news reporting, advertising and public relations and through the unconscious absorption of capitalistic values by creators and consumers in all the above aspects of the culture of everyday life. (Berger, 1991, p.37).

This analytical approach was employed to answer the question whether political advertising tapes under analysis furthered the class struggle inherent in western world. Are those class struggles evident in the portrayal of white versus blacks, rich versus poor, young versus old and so on.

The use of overtly ideological language seems scanty even though there is ample evidence to suggest that the rhetoric of Bill Clinton tilted in favor of a centrist politician with a welfarist approach to governance. The issues that the campaign tapes dwelled upon such as protecting Medicare and Medicaid, need for more jobs, and more police to keep watch over the neighborhoods. In addition, there were promises of more teachers, to strengthen education and banning of assault weapons and tax cuts to provide relief to middle class. All of these were indicative of a welfarist government peddling populist agendas.

In a countervailing manner, there was an ideological conflict in the approach of Clinton's opponent who looked at governance and government differently. This was evident in some of Clinton shots that rebutted his opponent's stance. Dole was a vigorous campaigner for less government and putting people on the steering wheel of their lives. Too much government involvement in people's lives was costing too much money, Dole reasoned. This issue was what pitched the two candidates, Bill Clinton and Bob Dole on an ideological battle field, even though Clinton did so without being overtly ideological. It notable that a centrist politician, espousing an emerging consensual or majority is likely is likely to look non-ideological.

What made the battle less virulent was the fact that Bill Clinton's welfarist approach seemed to favor less government involvement and less spending than before. But he advocated achieving these goals in a way that the vulnerable in the society were provided with safety nets and basic protections to ease their pains. Bill Clinton's ideological language reflected a somewhat right-of-center political program with a human face, as opposed to the rather harsh and brazen approach of his opponents.

There was, therefore, an appearance of convergence of ideological positions in which Bill Clinton and Bob Dole seemed to be saying the same thing using different styles. There was a shift, not just in style but also in language, in the way Clinton steered the Democratic Party away from the Left to the center of the ideological spectrum.

The shift to the center was necessitated in Britain and the United States by the search for new voters who may have become tired of the long conservative hold on power. The middle class, the social group to which Blair directed his election promises accounted for about half of the British electorate. (Time, April 28, 1997).

In the United States, Bill Clinton broke away from the ranks by talking about deficit cuts, free trade, and smaller government, all strong points for the right-wing Conservative Party. This ideological drift began in the United States and Britain around early to mid-70s following large-scale disillusionment with the left. The right wing market populism began to gain currency.

In Britain, Tony Blair ditched the leftist party's idea of public ownership and pledged to continue Thatcher's privatization policy. Tony Blair has been accused of betraying his traditional constituency on the left for the sake of power. As a result of this move, "they achieved office by making the privileged metropolitan elites feel good about themselves." (Reid, 1997, p.86).

The ideological shift in Britain was of more profound effect than the shift of the Democratic Party in the United States. This was because unlike the American Democratic Party,

> Labour was genuinely socialist...It is precisely because the Labour Party's belief in socialist economic solutions has long been so strong that any attempt to alter it must have an equally intellectual force. (Foreign Affairs, March/April, 1997, p. 45).

Clinton merely re-invented the Democrats as a centrist party. (p.45).

Verbal Codes: Synchronic analysis

Applying structuralist methods in the analysis of television ensures that a rigorous and accurate criticism is made possible. Structuralists use binary oppositions as one of its tools to define meanings in communication. The work of Structuralists depend on finding meanings that are embedded in any form of text, be it a feature-length movie or cartoon programs. This is dependent on how well the structures of the units relate to each other to make meaning-making possible. According to Allen (1992), "the meaning of each sign within a text derives from its relationship to other signs in the same system." (p.51).

In political advertising where one candidate tries to outdo the other by drawing contrasts in terms of their capabilities and achievements, structuralism can profitably be used for analysis. Structuralism is established on the principle that "units of any system have meaning only by virtue of their relations to one another." (p.51). One of the tools used by Structuralists is binary oppositions.

Therefore the text of the political campaign messages of Bill Clinton, were defined by binary oppositions. He portrayed himself as a caring and welfare-oriented candidate and depicted the opponent as an uncaring, insensitive candidate. Bill Clinton in his commercials created a different image of himself to contrast with that of Bob Dole and Newt Gingrich. This ensured a form of distinction, whereby contrasts can be drawn or "difference out of the undifferentiated." (Stillar, 1998, p.109).

The nature of the 1996 campaigns made it ideal for binary opposition. Not only did the candidates try to outdo each other by differentiating themselves from their opponents, words and expression were used to reinforce this. Binary oppositions that can be identified in the texts include young and old, a key campaign issue was that Bob Dole was too old to be president. Another paired opposition caring/uncaring, was constructed by Bill Clinton's campaign messages where they indicated staunch support for Medicaid and Medicare, services which his opponent wanted slashed.

Clinton presented himself as a progressive leader as against the "gangster" attitude of the Republican Congress. Other pairs were trustworthy versus deceitful, proven qualities versus unproved qualities, achiever versus non-achiever, youthful and energetic versus old and spent, forward-looking and optimistic against reflective and pessimistic.

Clinton presented himself as a candidate who epitomized the positive qualities while his opponent was associated with negative ones. Every one of these oppositions imply power struggle, contest and ideological warfare. It was obvious that any reader of the texts, especially the prospective voters, would notice how the text compelled them to identify with these contradicting sets of qualities. It made it easier for them to make a judgment on the candidates.

In scene after scene, these oppositions helped people determine which of the two candidates to vote for. The oppositions helped to establish that one candidate was what the other one was not. Whereas the duo of Dole and Gingrich were presented as less presidential-looking as possible, Clinton remained the object of authority and power, packaged in as presentable a manner as politically possible.

Color and image quality were also significant features that helped in the analysis of shots and scenes. For instance, any reference to Bob Dole and Newt Gingrich were fuzzily presented in black and white as opposed to the full rich color presentation of Clinton. In all of the shots analyzed, Bob Dole's image did not appear alone for a reason, to establish an association between him and the less-respected and controversial Newt Gingrich. This ploy was used to establish a relationship by association. It encouraged viewers to link Bob Dole with Gingrich and one could remember that Gingrich at that time was synonymous with confrontation, government shut-down and against senior citizens.

The importance of using binary oppositions becomes clear when one considers how the contrasts and oppositions carefully constructed between candidates force voters to make consequential political and voting decisions with great impact on their social and economic lives. Of course, choices are often influenced by each voter's social position in the class-structured society. The interpretation of these oppositions by potential voters was dependent upon where one belonged in the social scale and where one wished to be. This is what post-Marxist scholars like Gramsci (1971) refer to as the unending class struggle. A range of factors such as income, gender, race, social and political status play significant roles in the ascription of meanings to texts.

All capitalist societies are full of images conveying a sense of inequality with contrasts in wealth and deep poverty. In a ritualistic manner, politicians capitalize on voters' desires for egalitarian ideals during election campaigns with a promise that inequalities shall come to an end. Voters thus become objects of deceit in the process as the promises of today, soon to become disappointments, quickly become the campaign sound bites of tomorrow's election. The people are often the sacrificial lambs in the political gamesmanship. The dominant class, a privileged group to which the political class belongs, still controls the fate of the majority. Political campaigns are just part of the hegemonic ploy by which the few control the majority.

Verbal Codes: Communication Acts

The communication acts were determined by following Searle's (1969) format for analyzing speech acts. Each of the campaign shots analyzed was placed in categories that are common to most political advertising campaign text or talk. The categories included representatives, directives, commissives, expressives and declaratives.

Representatives included truth claims used in communication acts. In the case of Bill Clinton, representatives were used in most of the shots as a result of the negative campaigns that were used by both parties and their candidates during the 1996 campaign period. "The president's seven-year balanced budget protects Medicare..." "The president cuts taxes and protects our values." "The president proposes a balanced budget protecting Medicare, education, the environment, but Dole is voting NO." These were some of the claims in the shots.

Representatives included the rebuttals, denials or those references that sought to clarify or re-emphasize an issue as truthful. Many of such representatives were identified in which accusations, counter-accusations, and denials were used as negative speech strategies in the campaigns. Indeed, the 1996 political advertising has been referred to as the most negative in the history of political advertising in America. (Kaid, 1998).

Truth claims were also used by Bill Clinton to refute the allegations of tax increase on middle class income group, increase in teenage smoking, the MTV expose of his confession about smoking marijuana. Others were allegations of ineffective drug policies that resulted from porous border controls and the prevalence of drug use by teenage Americans. Bill Clinton used statistics to clarify these allegations.

At another level called pragmatics, Bill Clinton used the incumbency factor to full advantage. He used pronouns to convey an air of authority and position himself in front of the audience as a likable, yet distinguished leader, by producing social and political space between him and his audience. Like many accomplished orators, Clinton also uses pronouns such as "we," "I," "my," and "they." In one of the shots, Bill Clinton said, "We can make real welfare reforms a reality in the lives of the American people." He also said, "I said I will end welfare as we know it...." He interspersed his sentences with phrases like, "I can say this" and "let me tell you" to convey a sense of strength, confidence and authority. They also compelled the audience to focus on what was about to be said, and lent credence to his statements by reinforcing the dialogue between the leader and the led.

This use of pronouns enhanced the process of reinforcement and served to "coerce hearers" into paying attention. It also served to legitimize the speaker while at the same time de-legitimizing the opponent. These pronouns were effectively used in the longer infomercials much more than in the 30-second shots.

The verbal style adopted by Bill Clinton asserted his authority and reflected the fact that he was in a position of state power. There were flashes of pseudo-orders and muscle flexing which were characteristic of incumbents to legitimize their positions, re-establish superiority over challengers and win confidence through the flaunting of official status. Examples of pseudo-orders were "The Congress must agree to balance the budget without hurting American people." "The president says give every child the chance for college."

In the application of what Chillon and Schaffner (1997) referred to as commissives, Bill Clinton resorted to offering promises, offerings that were meant to convince the voters of his commitment to their causes. Commissives included promises, threats and offerings which were better made by the incumbent, especially by a leader like Clinton with high approval ratings.

Promises included statements like, "I am ready to meet tomorrow and give the American people their balanced budget." Also, "we can make real welfare reforms a reality in the lives of the American people." Threatening tone was also noticed in some statements like, "I will veto any bill that cut Medicare benefits, education or harms the environment."

Narrative analysis

Narrative analysis has ceased to be the exclusive preserve of literary critics who are noted for using this approach to unlock literary knowledge. Narrative theory's frontier has extended to such scholarly disciplines as anthropology, folklore, psychology and sociology. Qualitative researchers and professionals in medicine (psychiatry and psychoanalysis (Schafer, 1992) have also taken a cue (p.6).

Narrative analysis was used in this study to identify features in the patterns of speeches of President Clinton and Prime Minister Tony Blair. Presidential elections, a long and ritualistic process, are established as a continuing story, each told in a unique way and easily prone to different interpretations. In political advertising where heroic deeds of candidates are amplified along with other accomplishments, politicians employ discursive practices with which they get their stories across. Such practices include tales of humble beginnings, love of nation, service to humanity, values and duty. Individual landmark events are "organized and integrated" with unique narrative techniques, even though they originate from the larger symbolic system.

To every reader of a narrative, there is a unique meaning attached to the text. In essence, a narrative by its nature is "plurivocal", that is, "open to several readings and to several constructions." (Reissman, 1993, p14). A narrative has a broad definition and scope that it can incorporate anything and everything that seeks to provide answers to a question. For example, "what happened next?"

Narrative analysis essentially sheds light on how a story is told, and its two components are the story itself and the discourse in which the story is told. In other words, "the story is the *what* in a narrative that is depicted, discourse the *how.*" (Chatman, 1978, p.19). To adequately apply narrative analysis to a text Chatman suggests the delineation of its three components namely, event, character, and detail of setting. (Berg, Wenner, and Gronbeck, 1998, p.141).

Narrative analysis was employed to capture how the two leaders enabled us to make sense out of their experiences, how their attention to, and omission of certain details in their stories served to convey meanings to their audiences. (Reissman, 1993, p.4). The video tape analysis allowed for the study of the use of para-language styles like nuances, facial or body movements, dress format, tone, pitch and communication reflexes which are prone to various interpretations because they are culture bound.

For a narrative or a story to have coherence, the experience being related must be organized in a meaningful way for the whole world to be able to make meaning out of it. "Narratives are representations which structure perceptual experience, organize memory, segment and purpose-build the very events of a life." (Bruner, 1987, p.15). It is also said to be "the principle by which people organize their experience in, knowledge about, and transactions with the social world." (Bruner, 1990, p.35).

Narrative criticism should necessarily devote attention to three elements namely: conflict, reversal and resolution. The conflict being the struggle faced by the hero, the reversal is the change of fortunes for the hero or the villain, while the resolution is the anti-climax where the conflict is resolved. This study identified the narrative functions of each scene or frame, the themes, as well as the values in the narratives.

Essentially, the narrative analysis sought to identify metaphors, themes, metonyms, allegory, frames, explanations surrounding the settings, plots of the messages, and use of allegory and symbolism. It also defined the tone, voice, and pitch, as well as climax and video "shots" within the campaign video tapes.

Political candidates' campaign films constitute a unique showcase for story telling and may often be interpreted as a form of extended drama. Bringing input from life experiences of selves and others, politicians narrate how the past, their experiences in public and private lives, can be applied to make the future better for all. There is often a recurring use of life's metaphors to tell a story.

Propp's (1928) pioneering work is often referred to as the signpost to all narrative theory. He offered 31 functions commonly found in all narratives. Levi-Strauss (1967), in a follow-up study, shifts emphasis to analysis of text that examines binary oppositions. Whereas Propp emphasized sequence, Levi-Strauss emphasized opposition. Where else can one encounter such binary oppositions in large numbers other than the battle-field of political advertising campaign?

Levi-Strauss's work was evidently helpful in this study. Saussure in his landmark study "posthumously published in 1915' (Berger, 1991) drew a distinction between synchronic and diachronic analyses. Whereas synchronic analysis looks at paired oppositions embedded in the text, diachronic analysis centers on the chain of events.

Three components of narrative criticism were identified by Timmerman (1996) as crucial to giving meaning to a story. These are the plot, characters and values. All these are crucial also to the elements of narrative form, that is, conflict, reversal of fortune and resolution.

Following Timmerman's steps, the campaign tapes of Bill Clinton and Tony Blair were analyzed by determining their function, which was to persuade voters, then the narratives were broken down into elements. These elements were the plots, characters, and values. In the last step, the narratives were synthesized into a composite text, looking out for the following: allegories or metaphors in the stories with symbolic significance, dramatic irony, frame, place, plot, points of view, symbolism, theme, tone, climax, exposition and shot.

The analysis sought to answer questions such as: what stories did the commercials tell of candidate's heroism, of humble beginnings, accomplishments, and service to humanity. Did the political commercials feed off each other thus reinforcing the mythical essence of political rhetoric' Did a "culture grammar" evolve in the narratives leading to the assumption that a political advertising narrative common to the two countries is evolving?

The messages were embedded in the stories, which were told with the purpose of establishing a connection with the audience. Establishing a rapport with the audience through attention catching stories ensured that a communication bond was struck. Such narratives centered on heroism, facing challenges in the face of threats, courage and hope. Clinton boasted of leading the American people for four years during which economic growth was unparalleled.

The story was also told of Clinton, the brave, who was able to contain the action of a hostile Congress by vetoing unpopular bills that would have cut Medicare and Medicaid. He was the center of those stories, the hero, who surmounted all obstacles to fight the enemies on the opposing side.

The larger narrative of Bill Clinton's political life contained smaller stories of heroism of ordinary individuals, like survivors of criminal attacks, especially policemen who were felled by bullets, a mother of a disabled child faced with the ordeal of having to find life-saving treatment, or the testimonials as told directly by those involved in heroic acts. All of these corroborated the message of the Democrats that they are human, they had weaknesses and strengths. Bill Clinton was the hero in almost all the shots.

However, it was significant to note that other people too were offered the opportunity to relate their stories. For instance the testimonial by Lt. Randy Beane, a police officer from Dayton, Ohio, won the viewer's sympathy as his narration brought home the issue of violence in our society Officer Randy offered an eye-witness account of how his partner was gunned down by criminals. Also in a moving story of heroism, Sergeant Rodriguez narrated his story of his close encounter with death. "I was just terrified, that was it. I thought that was the last day of my life." He was shot at five times but survived the ordeal.

In all of these narratives, Bill Clinton was portrayed as the "deus ex machina", a type of magical machine, the God's ordained president who had answers to all the people's predicaments. His policies, either already activated like the Brady bill, or proposed like the welfare reforms, served to resolve the climax in the narratives. Those citizens who volunteered for testimonials served as the characters in some of these narratives.

Bill Clinton's presidency could be portrayed, using Vogler's (1972) approach, as the hero's journey. As a young president, who is well liked, even if not fully trusted, would be allowed by Americans to rule for four more years even if they could not trust him with their kids! Compared with his opponent who paraded a clean moral slate, it seemed that all the odds were against him. The antagonists were Bob Dole and Newt Gingrich with the White House, the ultimate choice prize. All of these are tied together with the metaphor of politics as a battle-field, with Bill Clinton leading the citizenry to the battle.

There were common themes running through all the narratives-that of a heroic president who wanted to serve his people for four more years. The plot centered on the agenda of the Republicans to stop Clinton from doing job, the people's job. The heroic triumph was in ensuring that the opponents failed to win the elections.

This was closely linked to the ritualistic element of election campaigns in which principal actors in elections are offered in sacrifice "as the regenerative ritual" that ensures that groups within the society endure. (Marvin, 1994, p.265). "By feasting on the sacrifice, the community is nourished and reconstituted." (p. 265). The narrative of election is thus described as "disorder redeemed by sacrifice." (p. 266).

The language of the narrative was filled with verbal appeals that exploited the stimulation of the audience's fantasy. There was "the feel good factor" based on the good economic indices that were flaunted in most of the campaign commercials. The audience members were encouraged to see themselves as deserving of the booming economy and as such, to reward themselves by voting for the Democrats once again so that the good days will continue.

This narrative strategy was probably applied in contrast with the opponents' approach of peddling fear and anxiety in their narratives. They predicted that Medicare funds would run out in years and that the economic bubble will burst if drastic cuts were not implemented in the mandatory spending areas like Medicare and Medicaid. Clinton allayed the fears of the electorate that had been heightened by the opposition candidate.

Clinton was able to use a unique style of delivery that appealed to human ideals and noble aspirations. His emphasis was on those issues that appealed to the middle class voters. Rather than look back at the glorious past like his opponent, Bob Dole, he paid attention to what lay ahead, targeting the concerns of the middle class American voters.

Essentially, Clinton used certain symbols to rally support of a diverse group of voters by addressing their problems. He targeted women, especially working women, children, the elderly, the law enforcement agents, legal immigrants, and working Americans and addressed issues like education, tax cut, minimum wage increase, and family leave, that are of interest to all these groups. Through practiced delivery, he was able to make the voters see their collective fears, aspirations, anxieties and frustrations through the symbols identified in the shots,

Tonal inflections and pitch fluctuations in the audio components of the tapes aligned with the messages, for emphasis, sometimes heightened the solemnity of the situation. Issues like welfare reforms, family leave, drug control and Medicare were featured in solemn tone to connote sobriety and seriousness.

Semiological analysis

Many research works with a focus on the analysis of political communication that use broad framework to categorize elements such as genre or issue, image, or stylistics fail to do justice to the subject matter. "Rather, these elements should be broken down into a set of elements or signs." (Biocca, 1991 p.18). Political advertisements need to be fragmented into words, sounds and images which clearly elucidate the totality of the messages.

The research method that fragments communication into words, sounds and images was pioneered by a Swiss linguist, Ferdinand de Saussure and an American, Charles Pierce. This method is centered upon meaning generation in signs or how meaning can be derived from texts, especially films, television, and music. The popularly accepted notion is that texts are made up of signs that we use in combination to produce meaningful messages.

The primary objective of semiotics is to determine how meaning is created, and thereafter find out what the meanings are (Seiter, 1987). Saussure identified two broad components, the signifier, which is the sound image and the signified, the concept represented.

Semiotics focuses on the generation of meaning and how that meaning is conveyed. (Berger, 1991, p.5). Human communication is made up of signs, comparable to a system of writing which are representative of something in some respect or capacity. These signs which make up communication have a life of their own and semiotics is "the science which studies the life of the signs." (p.6).

Semiotics is something present in communication which stands for something that is absent, for example, a cross represents Christianity, rose symbolizing love or affection, flag representing nationality or national identity, and so on. According to Barthes (1973), signifiers may be perceived as stable because a word or a picture may appear so, however, the meanings that may be attached to them can be unstable. Barthes (1957) also dwelled on myths as "a form of speech, a mode of signification..." (Randazo, 1993, p.30). Advertising is a form of mythologizing. Clinton used political myths to re-live the dreams of our forefathers in his reference to the constitution. He also created a myth around the 20th century as the millennium of hope and abundance. The fantasies created by images of a perfect society conveyed the notion that everything was rosy and in order. This was effectively done by evoking archetypal imagery of the various groups in the society. The average American middle-class worker, the single mother on welfare, the young teen who is about to pick up smoking, and the gallant police officer who was shot while on duty, all fall into the universal realm of those the new Democratic Party is appealing to. In all of these, "mythology helps people in their struggle to understand the universe and their place in it." (Randazzo, 1993, p.47).

Meanings are not static. They "change across time and setting."(Vande, Wener and Gronbeck, 1998, p.94). Fiske (1987b) provides a cautionary acknowledgment to this observation by referring to the likelihood of conflicts in generating meaning from the text, especially between the "forces of production and modes of reception," p.14).

Signs could be iconic, indexical, or symbolic. Iconic signs are those which have structural representation, similarity or resemblance between what is present and what is absent. Pictures or the drawing of an object are good examples of this. Symbolic signs are those with arbitrary relationship between the signifier and the signified. An example is the white wedding gown which symbolizes purity or virginity. Indexical signs are those which prod us to infer meanings from the symbol or object, for example the bowler hat and umbrella as a dress form for the British. (Leeds-Hurwitz, 1993, Berger, 1991, Berg, Wenner and Gronbeck, 1998).

The transcribed tapes were analyzed to detect any visual signs that represent something not made obvious in the video tapes. Semiotics is an appropriate tool in unraveling inter-cultural meaning. The use of these methods stems from some assumptions that communication which occur between human beings are made up of signs and symbols.

For instance, in the video tapes analyzed, metasigns were used to determine what social markers identified the people presented in the video. "Metasigns are sets of markers of social allegiance (solidarity, group identity and ideology) which permeate the majority of texts." (Hodge and Kress, 1988 p. 80).

Biocca's (1991) observation is notable when he says, understanding verbal language leaves analysts with little help to fully unravel the content of television messages, not the least political messages. There is a close link between symbols and its effect on power. Politicians compete to outdo each other in the scramble for the most impressionable political symbols, hence political advertising. "He who defines the symbolic terrain wins." (p.4).

Drawing deep-seated meanings from texts cannot be said to be complete without examining the relationships between the elements contained in the texts. Using synchronic analysis, it was possible to bring out those patterns of binary oppositions embedded in the text. This work which was done by Saussure (1966) and Vladmir Propp (1928) provide useful models of analysis using semiotics.

The importance of binary or polar oppositions in analyzing texts cannot be overemphasized especially because the relationship between the production of meaning in language is dependent upon opposition. (Berger, 1991, p.18). Saussure (1966) was quoted by Berger (p.18) as saying that, "in language, there are only differences." All human communication in the form of texts, is comprised of a "systematic and interrelated set of oppositions..." (p. 18).

The texts were, therefore, analyzed under three broad categories: verbal, visual, and acoustic codes. These categories were proved effective in addressing all the aspects of analysis that this study planned to accomplish. This is a replication of a similar categorization used by Berg, Wenner and Gronbeck (1998).

At the level of visual codes, how colors played meaning-making roles in the texts was examined. This was done to resolve the importance of color orientation, and how this contributed to making shots simple or complex, what objects and symbols were captured in the frames, both in the foreground and the background, as well as what icons were included to convey meanings to the overall picture. Colors have been identified to play a very crucial role in adding meanings to visual images, especially in political advertising. A blurred color presentation of an opponent serves to portray him or her in a less than impressive light and such techniques play a role in voter perception.

Williamson (1978) notes that color helps tell a story as well as provide oral connection, and if effectively used, can connect objects with other objects, as well as objects and person. (p.22). In this study, color was analyzed to determine how it was used for differentiation, and to make one candidate stand out and the other less visible. Use of colors to represent the symbols that the parties and the candidates were noted for, was also examined.

Berg, Wenner and Gronbeck (1998) break the analysis of visual codes into two segments, separating color, framing, complexity versus simplicity in visual codes, from the complex meaning systems like emotionality. (p.97). They go on to identify the acoustic codes which include auditory signs, paralinguistic cues, spatial organization of sounds and auditory echoes. All these components were used in the study to uncover the meanings in the campaign styles of the two politicians. The approach in which a number of research techniques are employed, is not only ideal for textual analysis, it is indeed very helpful in a comparative work such as this.

Morreale's (1991) study provided a useful model for this study because it went beyond mere semiological analysis to rhetorical analysis. Morreale claimed that semiological analysis used in isolation proved problematic when studying non-verbal images. (p.96). Textual frame analysis helps our understanding of "how context, source, text, and audience interact." (p.96). Frames also help in organizing and coherently organizing our experiences.

The basic unit with which Morreale began the analysis was from the level of frames, that is, "the organizational principles that govern interpretations of events." (p.20). These are sometimes dependent upon our expectations and experiences as viewers. The author provided a combination of theories unbounded by disciplinary frame, though rooted in rhetorical criticism.

This gave credence to the fact that meanings of texts cannot be determined or exhausted by just looking at it from a singular perspective. Perhaps one aspect of

Morreale's study, which was found very useful in this study, is in the area of identifying cultural myths. Morreale argues that myths are clichés which define moral community, and "mythic symbolization can be true, illusory or both." (p.46). A definition with some depth brings the issue into better focus. Frith's (1997) definition provides a clearer perspective on the importance of myths to any group of people. "They are preexisting, value-laden sets of idea derived from a culture and transmitted through various forms of communication." (p.11).

These mythical frames facilitated the understanding of those deep-seated messages that are being conveyed to the electorate. Whereas Morreale identified the myth of rebirth in the study of a film on Ronald Reagan, this study identified those of Bill Clinton and Tony Blair.

Mythical symbols "establish links between the individual and the political order as well as the synchronization of diverse motivations." (Elder and Cobb, 1983, p.1). They serve as mirrors through which the voters see themselves reflected in the issues being discussed. Such symbols become rallying points for support from groups of people who share similar fears, anxieties, dreams and frustrations. (Elder and Cobb, 1983 p.17).

Mythical invocation of symbols serve to stimulate in voters a form of reassurance for them as a group who share similar "identity, life-style or set values." (p.17). Such symbols may include issues on abortion, welfare, unemployment, health or education. Politicians have been acknowledged to "use dramatic symbolic gestures to assuage the anxieties and passions of prospective voters". (p.18).

Whereas ideological analysis of discourse seeks to explore the battle ground of class conflict presented in the discourse, the importance of non-verbal cues in political advertising is crucial to the allocation of meaning to televisual messages. "Face is the primary site for interactionally important cues and expression of emotions." (van Dijk, 1985 p. 213). Meanings can be generated not just by facial expressions, but also by other visual behavior such as eye movements, direction of gaze, eye contact, sweaty forehead, physiological changes like blushing and sweaty face. Discourse analysis in the study of texts "allow for the study of language in a social context which makes it socially relevant." (p.4).

The importance of applying semiotics in the analysis of political commercials rests upon the importance of this approach in interpretation in communication. For any form of communication to be interpreted successfully, especially 30-second commercials, those units of meanings contained in theme have to be deciphered. These are embedded in what Saussure refers to as "the referents" and the "interpretant." The referents refer to the sign and the interpretants are what we use to define the sign. According to Allen (1992) Umberto Eco defined a sign as "everything that, on the grounds of a previously established social convention, can be taken as something standing for something else." (p.35).

For these reasons, signs like the national flag, the Capitol and the Oval Office which were featured many times invoked the spirit of nationhood and nationality. Clinton in all of his appearances in the commercials had the flag in the background. The symbolic role of the flag in the national life was also evident in the scenes where fallen heroes like policemen killed in the line of duty were being laid to rest. The flag represented the state authority and national identity. Also effectively used to convey meaning was the White House and specifically the Oval Office to symbolize authority and to legitimize the incumbent, Bill Clinton.

Beyond this, the Capitol Hill, the seat of the Legislative arm of government was featured in almost two-thirds of the shots. The relevance of the image of the Capitol Hill was perhaps based upon the importance of the legislators, the occupants of The Capitol, who would deliver on the promises being made by Bill Clinton.

In a carefully selected fashion, the signs seemed tailored to add meanings to the graphical messages that were conveyed in the shots. In another scene, the Statue of Liberty, the essence of the American dream of freedom for all, was most potent and powerful. This was employed to invoke the feeling of collective aspiration on the part of the American people.

Significant also were the references to the Constitution, the legal framework on which the political life of America depended. Instruments of office like the gavel for the Speaker of the House, the president's pen, presidential seal of office, all conveyed images of authority, power, control and leadership.

Other significant symbolic signs were the cradle and the babies to depict regeneration, future and hope. On the other hand, the images of the elderly conveyed messages of the past, the glorious old days, a call to duty on the part of the younger generation to look out for the vulnerable elderly in our midst.

In almost all of the shots where Bob Dole and Newt Gingrich were shown, they appeared in the foreground while the Capitol Hill was in the background. The Capitol represents the bastion of American law and democracy. The building may be said to represent all that America stands for, freedom, equality, rule of law, democracy and accountability. It was here also, that Newt Gingrich held the whole country hostage with the shut down of the government. The image was a significant reminder to the electorate.

In a few shots, there were references to the Constitution, the articles from which government derived its powers, duties, responsibilities and limitations. These also conveyed a message of sacredness of America's democracy and rule of law. So are other symbols of authority like the Oval office, the flag, Statue of Liberty, the gavel, cradle and the baby.

Visual codes: Orientation

Color: Color was effectively used to convey meanings in the sense that they "provided basis for connection or connections unstated by the verbal part of the advertisement." (Williams, 1993, p. 20). In the case of Bill Clinton, color was used to tell stories beyond what verbal and graphic expressions could. Images of Bob Dole and Newt Gingrich were presented without color and made them appear unsympathetic, colorless and ineffective. The lack of color or the portrayal of opponents in black and white images sent messages beyond what was being said about them.

The color or lack of it evokes the social myth about darkness and light. Darkness is often said to be associated with evil, something hideous that can not be trusted. The removal of color from the images of Bob Dole and Newt Gingrich was to appeal to this sense of social myth-making.

In television advertisement color can enhance visual effects and draw viewers' attention. In of itself, the use of color may not seem particularly meaningful until it is correlated with something else. A colorful object has to be matched against a colorless one before the significance of the color becomes obvious. By helping draw contrasts, color distinguished images in the Clinton commercials. The color quality augmented by lighting effects enriched the images.

Scenes where references were made to the opposition were darker and had less in terms of lighting just as scenes that depicted unsightly situations had no lights and color. These included shots of kids who were smoking, policemen gunned down in the line of duty, toxic waste dump sites, among others. The darkness of the pictures coincided with the messages being conveyed

The relationships between the objects in the foreground and the background complemented each other. In all the shots in which Clinton appeared in the foreground, pictures of either the flag or the White House were featured in the background. Scenes set in the Oval Office also had the same setting where Clinton either sat or stood and the flag or the seal of office were in the background. All of these reinforced the aura of power and the strength of the incumbent president who has all the emblem of power at his disposal.

Bill Clinton in his appearances was able to amplify his messages with his emotion-laden delivery in the context that complex meaning systems like emotionality and the invocation of images of previously identifiable situations were provided. Like a political salesman he employed a semi-conversational style that made the messages sink easily into the audience's consciousness.

The Convention speech, more than the campaign shots, displayed paralinguistic cues. His speech was often punctuated with loud ovations that he had to gesture to the audience for their attention. When his speech touched on important issues like Medicare and Medicaid, curbing the wave of crime, or welfare reform, Clinton employed a soothing, rasping tone. The call for a better America on the eve of the new millennium was vintage Clinton, delivered in a tone of urgency. It was a clarion call of sorts, a very powerful call to action made with a metaphor of the "bridge to the 21st century," as if the journey to be embarked upon was a celestial one.

Tony Blair

Analysis of the campaign video tapes

In a fashion similar to what was done to the Clinton tapes, the video tapes of Tony Blair were analyzed based on the categories used by Berg, Wenner and Gronbeck (1998). Due to the lengthy nature of Party Election Broadcasts used in Britain, the number of shots or frames of reference was larger than those of the 30-second commercials employed in the Clinton campaign commercials.

For Tony Blair's campaign messages, seven different Party Election Broadcasts, with running times of about five minutes each, were analyzed. In addition to these, a speech delivered by Tony Blair at the Labour Party National Conference, running for an hour and thirty-five minutes, was included in the database for analysis. It was observed that similar to Clinton's video messages, Tony Blair did not refer to John Major with his title.

Attitudinal language used by Tony Blair in the video of the conference speech was unsparing of the Conservative Party and John Major. Attitudinal language included the usage of words that expressed positive or negative judgments about the principal actors. The nature of campaigns makes them prone to the use of negative attitudinal language. This is especially so because political advertising seeks to sell the positive qualities of a candidate while exposing the negative qualities of the opponent.

In the Labour Party tapes, the attitudinal language used vilified the Tories for the type of administration they offered the British people. "John Major's weak leadership would further reduce Britain's influence in the world..." In the conference speech, Blair said with derision, "Just say the word five more Tory years and you will feel your senses and reason repulsed by what they have done to this country." (See Appendix B, vi).

Tony Blair continued his vituperations on John Major by describing him as a minister "so weak, so utterly incapable of stamping his authority on the government he leads..." Blair said Major gave birth to "the first -ism in politics to denote not the existence of a political philosophy but the absence of one...Majorism, holding your party together while your country falls apart."

Nothing spoke louder than the graphic images presented in one of the shots in "The Mill" which was packaged in slow motion for effect. The Tory Party was captured during their national conference, clapping hands, chatting and cheering John Major. No audio was added. But for effect, the textual messages conveyed a negative portrayal of the Tories as a bunch of inconsequential people, a party of revelers who cared less for the daunting problems of the British people. This was powerful and effective.

Metaphorical language

There was a rich use of language that played a very significant role in adding layers of meanings to the tapes. The Labor Party hinged its campaign message on the metaphor of a new re-birth, a regeneration of sorts. The apt metaphor served the purpose of reminding the British people of the need for a change of government to something new, especially because the Labor Party had become rejuvenated with the revocation of Clause Four.

Prior to the elections, the opposing Conservative party had played on the age of Tony Blair, associating him with that of a baby. He was called "Bambi", Tony "Bla", "Bla" "Bla", mimicking the blabbing baby sound. Tony Blair's New Labour image was effectively used to link this baby image with newness, a re-birth from the old political ideals. The British electorate seemed tired of the old brigade in the two major parties and a new lease was added with the entrance of "Tony Bla Bla Bla!"

The Labor Party had alienated itself from the electorate, especially the business sector for a long time because of the rigid adherence to Clause Four, the heart of the Labor Party doctrine. This Clause frowned on private ownership of wealth. Predicated on the need for a change of baton, new leadership, new hopes and better future, the metaphor of a rebirth ran through all of the video tapes of Tony Blair. His youthful looks complemented the newness and vibrancy associated with something fresh.

Ideological use of language

At the level of ideological language, it was observed that the shots were not filled with ideological jargons often identified with the classic Labor Party. Political parties in Britain with much control and influence from labor unions hardly could avoid being rigidly ideological. This was not the case anymore. However, the testimonial provided by erstwhile Tory members were indicative of a shift in the ideological orientation of the traditional Labor Party.

The campaign messages hinged on traditional conservative themes like attitude to business, law and order and taxation. These were reinforced especially with the positioning of Tony Blair as a middle-class candidate and the use of conservative icons like the British bulldog, and the union flag. Labour Party's messages were based on the assumption that the Conservative Party had disappointed its followers and Labour cashed in on that by adopting conservative messages to attract new members while retaining hold on the old Labour members.

Issues that were often assumed to be the exclusive preserve of the Conservative Party and the accompanying rhetoric like less government, open-market economy (see Appendix B- Labor Business), balanced budget were all frequently used in the shots. The messages also crossed the party lines to include some of the very sensitive issues that were deemed of paramount concern to the middle-class voters.

The campaign combined the right-of-center ideological rhetoric with the traditional welfare -related issues of concern to the Labour Party by employing caring messages that emphasized the need for more jobs and better schools. It is right to say that in terms of ideological language, Tony Blair hovered around the center of the ideological spectrum, projecting a new sense of direction for the Labour Party. Tony Blair is often accused of running away with Tory policies by delivering the Conservative Party agenda with the Labor Party touch. No wonder the British press called him "Tony Blur." (*The American Spectator*, July, 1997).

The valuative language use included those remarks that related to psychological, legal, moral, religious, or aesthetic issues. Codes were embedded in the messages in a way that did not detract from policy issues. Though most of the Conference speech dwelled on aspects of values, they were applied as complement to the discussion of policy issues.

A clear example of valuative language use with focus on morality, was provided when Blair referred to the scandal which the Tory party was enmeshed in. The Tory Party on the eve of the elections was on the verge of being consumed by a rash of scandals on sex, homosexuality, lies, and corruption.

Psychologically, Labor Party played on the people's sentiments by sensitizing them to the scandals and directing their attention to them. Those scandals had profound impact on the internal structure and the entire fabric of the Tory Party, especially with regard to instilling discipline within the membership. Some of the messages did this by planting the fear in the electorate that another day for the Tories in government meant disaster for Britain. This fear appeal was effectively played upon in the shots. "If the Tories were given another five years, just imagine, they'd do as they pleased..." (See Appendix B, vii).

Synchronic analysis

Structuralists have argued that the "simplest way of marking difference is... by means of a binary opposition." (Hall, 1997). A concept becomes clearer or it derives its full meaning from its relation with its direct opposite. Words are what they are as much as they are what they are not. Night derives its definition and meaning because there is daytime, much as dryness is what it is because it is not the same as wetness.

The portrayal of Tony Blair was that of a youthful, vibrant politician, daring and energetic enough to wrest the power from the Tories in Britain. He was trusted enough to become the new leader after many years of Tory rule. What Blair signified went beyond what was seen in the images presented in the shots.

The structuralist approach was made popular by Saussure, who proposed that "a language consists of signifiers, but in order to produce meaning, the signifiers have to be organized into a system of differences. It is the differences between signifiers which signify." (Hall, 1997, p.32). Images in political campaign shots are noted for the use of binary oppositions, the manner in which candidates portray themselves can be best suited for a structuralist analysis.

In political advertising candidates enumerate those positive qualities which stand out over those of their opponents. Such "differences" in candidate qualities are discernible by drawing a set of "contrastive and distinctive features in the text". (Stillar, 1998, p. 109). This, therefore, brought up the need for identifying oppositions, those things that enunciated contrasts in images, objects or even situations.

For ease of analysis, the paired oppositions that were identified include youthful versus spent politician, morally upright versus immoral Tories, hope versus despair, truth versus lies, strong versus weak government, reliable versus unreliable, optimism versus pessimism, and so on. For everything that the Labor Party proclaimed itself to be, the Tory party was not. This was brought to the fore in the video clip on "Just imagine what would happen if the Tories got in again". Here, with the Tories clapping their hands in the frame, images of sand castle being washed away with the British flag, presented a lampoon of the entire Tory Party and what they represented. The entire Tory party was presented in negative light.

Codes used in the verbal constructions were also categorized for analysis. Representatives, otherwise referred to as truth claims, were significantly applied. This was used by Tony Blair to reinforce his campaign messages. The premise on which such claims were based depended on the fact that John Major had been identified as inept prior to the campaigns, and also surrounded by a bunch of incompetent allies.

Claims of truths served to pinpoint areas that needed re-emphasizing for clarity, especially as far as policy issues were concerned. For example, the statement made by Tony Blair that the Tories had introduced the highest taxes in peacetime history could be said to be a truth claim. Tony Blair also said, "we will be tough on crime and the causes of crime."

Truth claims are often easily alluded to by incumbents for campaign purposes than by their challengers. This is so for an incumbent candidate with high ratings in public opinion poll. However in the case of the challenging Labour Party, it was made relatively easier for Tony Blair because the Tories were put on the defensive all through the election campaign period. The Conservative Party was trying more to keep its members together than to focus on the campaign issues. The shots proved this well. It was less difficult for the Labor to show the electorate the effects of the truth claims because the Tories were confused and disorganized with in-fighting and rancor. For the Tories to refute the sleaze factor and claims to the truth simultaneously proved difficult.

Even though Tony Blair was yet to become the Prime Minister, as the leader of the Labor Party, he commanded the respect of his party men and women. His use of pronouns like "we in the Labor Party" "I, as the leader of the party", "I believe in the New Labor", attested to the air of authority that he created. Indeed in his conference speech, he referred to how he had been nicknamed "autocratic" by his opponents. Tony Blair's young age which implied lack of experience had been played upon by the opposition in the course of the campaigns. Therefore, he needed to brace himself with some authoritative use of language.

Commissives, according to Chillon and Schaffner (1997) are the promises, threats or such other offerings geared toward ensuring that the faith of the prospective voters was not lost. Tony Blair's messages were fraught with many statements that could be classified as commissives. These were to make promises of a better government, lower taxes, safer streets, smaller class sizes and so on.

He offered five pledges by which he wanted the British people to judge him. These are that class sizes will be cut to 30 for five, six and seven-year olds, fast track punishment will be ensured for persistent young offenders by halving the time for arrest and sentencing. National Health Services (NHS) waiting list will be cut by 100,000 patients and 100 million Pounds Sterling will be saved from red tape to save NHS. Also, 250,000 under-25 year-olds will be cut off welfare benefits and moved to work force. Additionally, income tax rates will not be raised while Value Added Tax on heating will not exceed 5 per cent. These pledges were given to reassure the voters that the Tories did not deserve their votes and the Labourites certainly did.

Threats and panic appeals were sometimes employed by Tony Blair. These included statements which instilled fear in the minds of voters, perhaps those in doubt of the New Labor, or those who had been disappointed with the Tories. To these groups of people, Tony Blair "threatened" dire consequences of voting in the Tories for another five years in a whole segment of his broadcast.

Narrative analysis

Delivered mostly in first person narrative style, Tony Blair used proxy narrators in very few of the shots for variation and delivery effect. This style enabled him to bring to the fore personal values, personality traits and his experiences to the campaign. His story was told in an eloquent fashion laden with emotion. He always spoke in well-constructed, seamless paragraphs" (*Time*, April, 28, 1997).

Tony Blair narrated the sad story of his father who had medical problems and how his family coped in the face of adversity. He portrayed a populist image of himself by situating himself in such a way that the ordinary folks could relate to him. He climbed down from the high pedestal of authority, verbally, and even physically to mingle with the prospective voters. He appeared casual in many of the scenes. Blair narrated the story of his childhood that, "When I was growing up, the family was strong, the sense of social responsibility was strong, crime was low, there was a sense of national ethos..."

The personal story of his life endeared Tony Blair to his audience. At about 10 or 11 years, Blair's father suffered a stroke. According to him, "all our lives changed after that..." It was very tough on him and all of us and my mother nursed him for three years and taught him how to speak again...He had to give up all his political ambitions." For the few minutes, he was able to create the archetypal image of a little boy who suffered adversity at a tender age but was able to survive. Every society would be able to relate to that heroic archetypal story. It was also a touching and emotional narrative.

Despite the length of the campaign shots, almost five minutes for each, except one that was 10-minutes long, his style of delivery and the life which he breathed into them, made less boring. There was a sense of cordiality and intimacy between him as the narrator and his audience. In the video clip, "Labour complete", Blair was presented in a most "presidential" fashion, as young, dynamic, never speaking from behind a desk..." (Howells, 1997, p.445). The tone was conversational. In some interview sessions, or "talking head" scenes which are often boring, Tony Blair brought some shine in them. His choice of words in answer to questions also suggested a conversational style, with a setting that matched the situation.

Tony Blair employed the use of repetition in his narrative style for emphasis. "We will respect family life, we will encourage and develop it...We will provide opportunities..." "We will cherish and enhance the environment, "we will change the law to make the Tories clean up." "We will be tough on sleaze and the causes of sleaze." These are some of the repetitions of the words, "we will." Repetitions serve not only to reinforce a point or add stress, they also guide the audience to pay attention to what is being said. They help attract and retain the audience's attention. This is often very effective in advertising as they aid memory recall and recognition.

He was either walking around, shaking hands, carrying babies, playing sport, or riding in a car or train, all indicating a middle-class conservative lifestyle. In one of the shots he was portrayed as a family man teasing his son about homework. It was a move to present him as a leader that the voters can relate to. The Tory Party had sought to demonize Tony Blair in their campaigns.

Even the interview sessions did not deviate from being issue-centered despite the semi-formal approach of presentation adopted. Broken down into units or scenes, each could pass for separate vignettes with well ordered meaningful components capable of forming a sequence of a larger story line or plot.

One important element was identified in how Blair's campaign broadcast harbored two levels of meanings, the manifest and the latent. Two examples can be identified here. In the clip "The Mill", there was a British bulldog, a "Churchillian icon." (Howells, 1997, p. 445), shackled by the Tories in power.

The bulldog as a British icon, is noted for resilience and aggression. Here in the clip, the bulldog is helpless, and inactive. It is tied down and in a deep slumber, ostensibly because of Tory's bad government. In a series of scenes, Tony Blair reels off his campaign promises like incantations to which the bulldog begins to react. First the bulldog opens its eyes. "We will be tough on crime and tough on the causes of crime", Blair offered. The bulldog rises. On the Labour Party's three priorities, "education, education, education," Blair seemed to be calling the dog back to life, back to reality...The bulldog breaks lose and heads for the direction of sunrise, an imagery that depicts future, hope and optimism.

Looked at closely, the British bulldog was made to represent Britain, a synecdoche of sorts. The old Imperial Power with the most powerful navy! The bulldog in a deep slumber and shackle depicted a potentially great power at its nadir, grounded by inept government and denied of its full potential. Tony Blair serves the purpose of the medicine man whose campaign promises restored hope for the British people. Britain will rise again, and it did as shown in the manner that the bulldog broke away from its shackle.

In another example in "The Mill 2," we are made to search for the levels of meanings in a sentimental story depicting the disappointment of the British people with the Tory Party's policies. Tom and Becky, his daughter, were archetypes of the average British voter. They were seen coming out of the hospital into the rain. It was 10 o'clock at night! The polls have closed for the day.

A cab appeared and both father and daughter are taken away. Remarkably, the cab driver, playing the role of some sort of angel, knows the names of his passengers and where they lived! He knew why they were in the hospital, Becky had a broken arm, and that they had spent six hours waiting for a doctor. The cab driver in a chat with Tom talks about the "terrible weather", which was not the rain but the government of the day! The driver said, "Tom, you've got to face it: the Tories have let you down."

Suddenly as the driver began to reassure Tom, the rain stopped. An upbeat mood is noticed outside as people began to fold their umbrellas. "That's why you've got to vote" said the driver to Tom. "Take it from me", the driver said to Becky, broken wings soon mend..." The driver develops white angelic wings and flies away. The magical touch was impressive. Not only were Becky and Tom back where they had been picked a while ago, the clock had rolled back for Tom to be able to vote! This was packaged with the effective use of a sophisticated filmic technique that carried meanings at many levels. There were archetypal characters, there was flashback and flash forward styles as well as the ability of one of the characters to foretell what was ahead.

Tony Blair was able to exploit to the fullest, a very partisan appeal because he tailored his messages to the middle class, comprising important demographic groups that often swayed British elections. He harped upon public policy and issues that the middle-class valued most and went all out to support him. Blair's attention was focused on issues paramount to this crucial demographic category.

Semiological analysis

At this level of analysis, it was observed that a multiple array of codes, signs and symbols were employed. These conveyed meanings beyond what the images presented. Manifest and latent meanings were determined in the shot "The Mill 1," where a bulldog was used to depict Britain. Noted for being tenacious, the bulldog used to depict Britain in this shot was, however, deeply asleep and snoring. This was the image of Britain under the Tories as presented by Tony Blair.

In another shot, Conservative Party members were shown holding their conference in a merry mood. There was no audio. However, the impression was that they had put Britain in danger by building a sand castle by the river. The castle was used to depict Britain along with the British national flag hoisted on it. Castles are common in Europe and they stand for safety, protection and strength. Representing Britain with a sandy castle was an oxymoron, yet powerful in its underlying message. All was not well with Tories' Britain.

There was the image of the British Bobby standing in front of the polling center. British Bobby, with their long caps and serious look represent constancy and timeliness. In public places like the entrance to the Buckingham Palace, the British Bobby's change of guards can be used to determine time of the day. These were some of the very powerful codes that were identified as being capable of conveying meaning at more than one level.

In the clip, "The Mill 2," the cab driver played the dual role of a driver and an angel. His cab driver role was representative of the hard working citizens while his angelic role was that of a concerned saint who wanted a miracle to happen on election day, which would happen if the Tories were voted out. In the role of the angel, he was able to change the clock backwards to allow new Labor party converts reach the polling stations before they closed.

In terms of production techniques, colors were effectively used for image enhancement. Williams (1993) described the use of color in video for expression and a myth-making process. Colors act as borders to differentiate between, and demarcate, two or more things. As a picture production technique, colors give identity and individuality to objects, and delineate objects from what they are not, by letting viewers see what they are, thus creating boundaries of divergence.

For example, in the shot "Locomotion," where John Major and his party members were the focus of attention, color was removed thus making the images less appealing than those of Tony Blair. There was an oral connection between the images and color presentation. The setting of the conference did not have any bright red colors that might be connected with the socialists or communism. As part of the new look, Labour had changed its color from pink to purple. In the choice of dress colors too, Tony Blair seemed more adventurous than his opponent, John Major, who wore dull colored suits and ties. In the clip "The Mill 2," Becky's dress was bright yellow, depicting bright optimism and youthfulness, all images with which the Labour wanted to be associated.

The seminal television debate between Richard Nixon and John F. Kennedy had been referred to as a debate that played a significant role in election outcome due to image projection through the use of color in dress. Even in black and white images, lighting could complement or detract from how an image is presented. Colors aid in sensitizing viewers by adding meaning to internal qualities. This is done by applying external techniques which appeal to the sensory organs of the viewers, the eyes. Colors speak volumes.

In the structure of the frames and settings, Tony Blair appeared in the foreground in most of the shots while the images in the background complemented rather than detract from his image, even when he was filmed in company of world leaders like president Mandela. Therefore, color could be said to have been effectively used for differentiation purposes in the shots. In political advertising as in product advertising, color may not be significant on its own, it is the correlation that color makes with other elements that adds significance to it. (Williams, 1993).

Tony Blair's tone was, no doubt, intense and at the same time charismatic. Being the challenger, he tried a little harder to be as convincing as possible. This could be explained by noting that there were no official emblems of authority that he could use to enhance the strength of his message. He, however, compensated for this with the vigorous paralinguistic codes like gesticulations, desk-pounding, roving head movements, especially at the party conference, where he surveyed the audience at intervals for acquiescence.

There was synchrony in the way verbal, textual, visual and audio codes fused into meaning making components. For instance in the only video clip that featured the Tory members, only textual messages, not even audio or verbal codes were employed. Despite this, the message spoke volumes when the slow-moving pictures of the party members were displayed with bold textual messages acting as the guide/unseen voiceless narrator. It was powerful in the sense that this showed that not only could pictures convey meanings, they could do so more effectively if complemented by textual codes even if without the audio.

For auditory effects, each video clip had the music theme of a British artist, Gabrielle, serving as reinforcement. The musical note and the lyrics were always interjected in the codes, be it verbal, visual or textual, for wholesome effect. Murray and Murray (1996) cited works like those of Bruner (1990), Gorn (1982), and Parker and Young (1986) which found links between music in commercials and affective and behavioral attitudes of viewers. This was no exception.

"Things will only get better...", the refrain in Gabrielle's chart-burster label rhymed effectively with the banner line of the Labor Party, "Britain deserves better...Things can only get better..." This was an adequate reinforcement to the

Labor Party messages. This created a complete interaction between the codes. At each level, verbal, visual and textual elements were consonant with each other in terms of themes and intended meanings.

Chapter VI
Comparative Critical Analysis

Comparing the two politicians at the linguistic level revealed that Clinton and Tony Blair were similar in their styles of reference to their opponents. Neither of the leaders did mention the titles of their opponents in any of their references. In the case of Tony Blair, it was obvious that as the challenger he never mentioned John Major never by his title as if the election results had been found out already and Major was no longer in power.

The use of negative attitudinal language in both cases was similar. Although Kaid (1998) had determined that the 1996 presidential election campaigns in America were the most negative in the history of American politics, it probably was the same in Britain. The scandals that surrounded the Tory Party made it an easy target for negative advertising, and Tony Blair was unsparing to say the least.

Tony Blair had used words like "incompetent" to describe John Major. "The Tories never did have the best vision for Britain', he said. Also, that the Tories were the "most irresponsible and incompetent managers of the British economy in the country's history." An explanation for Clinton's language could be traced to the similar attitudinal language choice of his opponent, Bob Dole.

Some of the clips in which negative language was used were rebuttal of something negative or personal that the Republican candidate had said. This was the case with the clip on tax cut, drug policing and border control which Dole had claimed Clinton did little or nothing about. Blair also complained of the rough tactics of the Tories who had resorted to negative campaigns close to the election time.

121

The two candidates focused on some issues that were of importance to the voters. Despite the negative content of Bill Clinton's video clips, salient issues were emphasized such that the voters could easily determine which of the two candidates they would cast their votes for.

It was observed that valuative use of language by Clinton and Blair was tailored to the needs of their target, the middle-class voters. There were similarities in the way they appealed to the sense of value of the middle-class voters. Duty to the elderly was emphasized, and so were the right of the children to quality education, and the citizens" to lower taxes, clean and safe environment as well as the issue of morality and accountability in government. They sounded eerily alike on those issues of values and morals.

In the use of metaphorical language, both candidates applied this in their clips for impact. Bill Clinton's use of the metaphorical language had similar impact as Blair's because the 21st century metaphor ran through the whole campaign while the metaphor of re-birth and newness did the same thing in Blair's.

The central themes of Clinton's campaign revolved around the metaphor of the bridge to the 21st century while Blair's youthfulness, newness and re-birth echoed all through his campaign. The 21st century was positioned as a fantasy journey to the dreamland, where everything will be made perfect. The bridge would facilitate this journey and Clinton called for "builders and engineers" to construct this bridge across time.

Tony Blair's metaphor of newness was predicated upon the changes that the Labour had witnessed. The party offered to the voters a new, young and vibrant leadership, a new structured party with brand new ideology, in search of new converts. Indeed, the messages were targeted toward new converts as much as to the traditional party faithful. Newness here depicts hope for the future. It is everything the old is not. It is the promise for a better tomorrow.

The newness of the party appeared to be beyond the superficial. It is the re-birth of a party and the Labor leadership promised the nation a new lease on life after 18 years of Tory rule. The party had been refurbished, had new converts from the ranks of the conservatives, and was new because it had been on the political fringes in Britain for 18 years. However, the newness could imply that Tony Blair, a younger generation politician would breathe new life into British politics.

Other commonly used metaphors included those that described Medicare as a program that was "withering in the vine" or the impasse between the Congress and the White House as a "tug of war" which called for a need to "protect America" as it was in danger of some sort. The war metaphor was sparingly used but it still had a significant impact in those areas where it was applied. Those metaphors served a cognitive role for conveying messages about a situation as realistically as possible both visually or verbally.

Where Clinton used metaphors, Blair applied coded and multi-layered signs to get his messages across. Blair veered away from the use of traditional visual clichés like the national flag, historical monuments or other insignia of office and used instead, symbols that conveyed deeper levels of meanings. His challenger role limited him on how much of official status or insignia he could be identified with.

An example of this dual level meaning was in the clip, "The Mill 2," where a cab driver played angel to archetypal characters, a politically disillusioned man and his daughter. (See Appendix B, xiv). He played the role of cab driver, narrator, and hero all at once. This clip was an effective narrative on its own. It told a story within a story using filmic device of multi-plot story line. Another effective example was the clip, "The Mill 1," where the snoring bulldog was used to represent Britain under John Major. (See Appendix B, vi)

The styles of delivery used by both leaders were a lot different. Clinton was masterful in the way he played on his tone and pitch to deliver his message with a massaging voice. Tony Blair seemed to have tried harder to strike a convincing pose in his style of delivery. His delivery was fast-paced, somewhat upbeat and racy and appeared a little too much in a hurry to convince his viewers. This may be due to the fact that Blair, unlike Clinton was the challenger and had a little bit more to say to win the voters' attention.

Tony Blair was more witty, especially during the conference speech. He interjected his speech with humor, calling himself names in self-deprecatory manner, "Bambi," "the great wise leader," "president for life" ostensibly given him by the Tories and the press. In some circles, he had been accused of being dictatorial and intolerant of opinions that did not tally with his. The audience laughed heartily time and again in the course of the almost 120-minute tape. Tony Blair fondly referred to his shadow cabinet members and joked with them as he delivered his speech.

In the Clinton speech, he was formal and struck a serious pose. Clinton wanted appeared as presidential as possible. It was obvious in his campaign commercials that he steered clear of controversies even though his opponents wanted to drag him in so as to expose him to criticisms. The very careful nature of Clinton's campaign served him well as a potent tool to shield him from the negative advertising campaigns of his opponent. He thus retained this mien that presented him as towering above the wrangling associated with dirty politics. In a nutshell, he conducted himself in a stately manner.

Besides, Bill Clinton was able to employ incumbency style, or what Trent and Friedenberg (1991) called the "Rose Garden Strategy of Symbolic Resource." This meant that Clinton exploited the advantage offered by the "symbolic trappings of the office" of the president on his campaign trail.(p. 65). As the clips showed, the signs and codes that were employed indicated that Clinton had transferred the ornate and the grandeur of office for full political mileage.

Blistered from scandals of various types and dimensions, it had been the hope of the Republican Party to exploit these setbacks to draw Clinton into the quagmire and use that to flush him out of office. That was why the campaigns were so negative, personal and caustic. It was more the aura of the office that established Clinton at a higher sociopolitical legitimacy than his rival, Bob Dole.

Aided by his own charisma, Clinton was propelled ahead of Dole in the polls and made his opponents look petty. His approach of towering over these scandals by distancing himself from all the squabbles around him was shrouded under the notion that he had a duty to the nation and the electorate. Clinton's staying power seemed to have rested on these qualities which he has exhibited time and again during his many episodes of scandals.

There was a more discernible chronological pattern in Blair's narrative style much more than was evident in Bill Clinton's speech. Whereas Blair embedded his messages with vignettes that added punch to his messages, Clinton resorted to chest-beating on his achievements in the preceding four years before the elections.

We heard stories of personal heroism from Blair while Clinton's heroism rested on official accomplishments. These included how he was able to bring unemployment and budget deficits down. His narratives centered upon what he did in office, not outside of it. He cleverly played within the court since the Republicans wanted to drag him out of it and play rough on his personal character.

One other narrative quality that Blair displayed was in his regular resort to repetitions for emphasis. He would repeat his promises with refrains like, "we will" do this and that, reeling off those promises by repeating "we will" at the beginning of each sentence. This was effective in compelling the audience to pay attention to him.

Para-linguistic codes were frequently and effectively employed by the two candidates. Tony Blair applied this perhaps displaying more outpouring in his approach than Bill Clinton. For instance, Blair did more table-banging, punching and cutting the air at intervals to emphasize his disdain for the Tories.

Bill Clinton remained presidential by appearing formal at all times while Tony Blair appeared in semi-formal wear, sitting at breakfast table with his family, playing soccer with kids, or playing tennis. The dress format of Blair in the commercials was very simple unlike that of Clinton. Except during the speech Blair dressed formally in suit. He was either in shirt and tie, or even sports wear as in the shot where he was seen playing tennis.

The portrayal of Tony Blair, the people's man, was effective for him because he was seeking acceptance and wanted to be identified as approachable. Clinton just let his credentials as incumbent speak for him. All he did was re-echo those dominant themes as often as he could.

To do this effectively, Clinton had resolved to the use of those symbolic codes that appealed to special groups of voters as a means of catching their attention. Women, minorities, middle class Americans and even young voters like college kids. Politicians have been known to use "dramatic symbolic gestures to assuage the anxieties and passions" of prospective voters. (Elder, 1983, p. 18). This was done by focusing attention on those issues that bind these people together, their collective fears and hopes.

There were evidently discernible similarities between the two leaders in the ideological language employed. This may have been the reason why both candidates were thought to be so much alike. They both campaigned on those key issues that appealed to the crucial voting groups within the two societies, namely, the middle class and women. They both campaigned on the platform of tax reduction, smaller classroom sizes, larger and better-equipped police to protect the people, drug free environment, and empowering women.

What made the similarities so obvious was that the two candidates were canvassing for votes from the same social class from a traditionally leftist political party. However, the rhetoric used was that of the traditionally rightist political party, or at least a centrist one. They both steered away from being ideologues, appealing instead to populist agendas that cut across rigid ideological divides.

Both Bill Clinton and Tony Blair effectively used the camera to enhance their likeability and credibility before their audiences. They were both close to the camera in almost all the clips. Kepplinger (1990) established that such closeness of the camera could influence the politician's acceptance by the viewers. This was especially so in the case of Bill Clinton and Tony Blair during the "talking head shots" or the infomercials, and the conference speeches, which captured longer sessions.

Biocca (1991) concluded that the closeness of the camera to the politician enabled the viewers read facial movements, which complemented verbal communication, and resulted in a positive evaluation of what the politician said. Nowhere was it better amplified than in the videos of Clinton and Blair that facial movements constituted a vital part of the message. What played to the advantage of the two leaders was their youthful looks which conveyed re-assurance rather than the despondent looks of their opponents.

More than Bill Clinton, Tony Blair put to better use his body movements, not the rigid type of a communicator who sat glued to a spot. The movement in space by a communicator serves to display his physical posture, vigor and agility. In all of the shots that Blair appeared in, he was either shaking hands, walking in the streets, playing with the kids, driven in a car or addressing an audience. He effectively used the approach sometimes called slice of life spot, that is, spots that showed a candidate in a greater depth, and real life situations. Bill Clinton put up the presidential air in all of his shots by either signing a document in his office, sitting behind his desk or addressing an audience. That took life away from the campaign commercials.

Bill Clinton used the name identification spots more effectively than did Tony Blair. He was able to crow about his achievements in the last four years before the elections whereas Blair was only able to identify the inadequacies of the opponent thereby augmenting his own credentials. When Clinton boasted of cutting budget deficit by half, saving Medicaid and Medicare, reforming welfare and cutting taxes for working families, Tony Blair insisted that Britain deserved a better life than they had under the Tories.

Besides, Blair was able to identify himself as a youthful challenger who is able to bring new vigor into the politics of Britain and Europe. He could not use the props of the presidency as Bill Clinton did in most of the spots. He had to import real life images to show him as a better man than his political rival and capable of winning the people's trust.

What was common to both candidates' campaign video clips was the fact that they used proxy narrators, who espoused the qualities of the two leaders for effect. Bill Clinton of course used this more often. In addition to this similarity was the use of testimonials from representatives of the different segments of the society. For instance, policemen gave testimony in Clinton's shots that the Brady Bill will ensure that guns will not end up in the wrong hands. Business-men and women testified for Tony Blair that doing business with Labor was no longer a risk as it was in the past.

The use of testimonials in ensuring that the candidates were identified and authenticated by certain segments of the population has become very popular in political campaign commercials. Such testimonials in the clips ascertained that the candidate was portrayed as supportive of inclusiveness in his political camp, especially when such testimonials were given by the ordinary man on the street, a member of a minority group, or specialized groups like the business sector.

More than Bill Clinton, Tony Blair applied music into his video clips for additional communicative purposes. The theme of the lyric rhymed effectively with the slogan of the labor Party. "Things can only get better", a popular song by a British pop artist, Gabrielle, was used as the refrain at the end of each shot.

It served the dual purpose of re-echoing the party's slogan as well as serving as a device to attract the younger generation that the music appealed to into the whole campaign message. This style also provided an avenue for interaction between verbal and acoustic codes for the purpose of reinforcement. Auditory echoes such as the theme of this popular lyric served to re-enact the feel-good objective of Tony Blair's message.

Both Bill Clinton and Tony Blair brought to bear a highly potent argumentative orientation that enabled them to sell their promises to the electorate. Even though the approaches employed are different in some spheres, the approaches used in their arguments, which was to solicit votes from the electorate, were still very successful judging by the caliber of opponents that they were pitched against. This explained why Bill Clinton was able to secure re-election in the United States despite his scandals but John Major could not do the same in Britain.

Most glaring in the pattern of speech was Tony Blair's frequent resort to repetition for emphasis, a style that Bill Clinton never used. Tony Blair used the slogan, "Britain can be better" so often as a refrain that the viewers could not possibly miss the impact it created. He also employed the use of repetition for emphasis when responding to the question of his three most important policy priorities. He responded, "education, education, education."

Whereas Blair used repetition for emphasis purposes, Bill Clinton employed the use of allegory revolving around his "bridge to the 21st century." All of the policy issues mentioned by Bill Clinton relied upon this proverbial "bridge" as if it was the connection between him and his audience. Overall, however, it was Tony Blair who applied allegory to more effective use than Bill Clinton. This was evident in the stories told in "The Mill 1," "Locomotion" and "The Mill 2" where stories embedded with multi-layered meanings were used to canvass for votes.

In all of Tony Blair's spots, there was a metaphorical story embedded. Each one complemented the other in the diffusion of meaning. Take for example the allegorical story used in the spot, "The Mill 1" (see Appendix B, vi), we saw the story line which was centered around a weak bulldog, sleeping and snoring, whereas the whole message was representative of a weak Britain that had become ineffective following the Tories' government.

The reason why Tony Blair could put together such spots with multiple levels of meanings was because of the time frame allowed for each election broadcast, almost five minutes, compared to Bill Clinton's 30 seconds. In that regard, the major purpose for Clinton was getting the message across as quickly as possible with the least number of words while Tony Blair could afford the luxury of a flourishing language embedded with multiple meanings.

Chapter VII
Discussions and Conclusions

Political communication, under which political advertising campaign falls, is evidently a very extensive area of research. This study is a contribution to the rich reservoir of knowledge in political communication. This book drew extensively from the wide array of literature in political communication. This was done by grouping the literature according to the themes they contained. A large segment employed the quantitative research method by measuring political adverting effects on voter perception, candidate image and voting behavior.

The choice of a qualitative approach in the analysis of comparative communication styles was made to fill a void that existed in political communication as few studies employed qualitative research methods. Most studies examined cause-effect angle of political communication using quantitative research methodology. This study thus looked beyond what quantitative studies could achieve.

A triangulation approach was employed, incorporating such theories as narrative analysis, semiotics, discourse analysis among others, in establishing if similarities identified in the campaign styles of Bill Clinton and Tony Blair were such that could make them clones of each other.

The analysis was conducted by employing the structured approach used by Berg, Wenner, and Gronbeck (1998). Each of the shots was analyzed under five broad categories, namely, Verbal codes with emphasis on linguistic acts, Verbal codes, with emphasis on communication acts, Visual codes, with focus on orientation, Visual codes, with focus on Semiotics, Visual codes, with focus on complex meaning systems, and Acoustic codes.

Campaign video tapes of Bill Clinton and Tony Blair were first analyzed individually using those categories listed above before they were compared for similarities and differences. A chapter was set aside for the analysis and comparisons. The following conclusions were, therefore based on those observations drawn from the analysis. Each of the research questions was answered based on the findings from the analysis.

It was established that the two leaders shared some similarities in their narrative styles even though these cannot be said to be significant enough to conclude that they shared the same narrative styles. The tone and the pitch of the narratives were a little different, both had stories to tell about themselves, their lives and accomplishments, but these were told in different ways. Tony Blair used a conversational style of communication while Clinton was formal in his narrative approach. Blair used repetition for emphasis, Clinton did not. Blair's narrative was fast paced and racy, Clinton's was not.

However, the general themes of the messages were similar essentially because they had the same groups of voters as primary targets. Issues of paramount interests to these groups seemed to coincide across cultures. Each in his unique way exhibited a cohesive structure of communication style. Blair employed an effective body language, with repetitive words and phrases for emphasis.

The research question on whether the patterns of the messages were reflective of similar political ideologies was, however, found to be true. Both candidates embraced issues that situated their political ideology right in the center of the ideological spectrum. Even the traditionally leftist Labor Party of Britain became born again under Tony Blair. Both cleverly steered away from those language choices that pigeon-holed them in the class of left wing radicals. They hovered ideologically in the center.

One could also answer the question of whether the British political communication styles were witnessing a process of Americanization as not entirely true. Going by Kaid's (1991) definition of "Americanized" political campaign style, one could say that the British political style has become "Americanized" especially concerning the emphasis placed on candidate image over party.

In the case of Tony Blair, there was an increased emphasis on candidate image over party dominance but "capsulated messages", another feature of American politics, was not frequently used by Blair. (Day, 1982, p.8). Capsulated messages are those short instantaneous messages suitable to the demands of television, sometimes called soundbites. In the age of television, political rhetoric has been transformed from the flowery language of old to the crisp, thirty-second succinct messages.

Kaid and Holtz-Bacha (1995) contend that the Americanization of campaign styles includes, "the predominance of images instead of issues, the professionalization of political actors in the development of media strategies" and the dominance of television in political campaigns. (p.9). Scammell (1998) wonders if globalization is the same thing as Americanization?

However, to assume that the British political campaign style does not have an identity of its own that is different from the typical American variety may be wrong. Tony Blair showed in his campaign a blend of styles in which issues were well articulated and they remained of paramount interest. Although candidate image was important, it did not supersede the discussion of political issues. Perhaps for the first time in the history of the Labour Party, a full 10-minute broadcast was devoted to the leader, shifting emphasis to the individual rather than the party.

Kaid and Holtz-Bacha (1995) insist that similarities may exist in some situations when a comparison is made between the political campaign styles in

America and other parts of the world. This is not to say that important differences do not exist. Such differences include those that border on "political structures and processes, in political culture and in media systems." (p.10).

The visual styles used by both candidates are somewhat different. These include locations used, settings, symbolic icons and other visually effective signs that convey meanings. Whereas Clinton used official icons to send his messages, Blair used the common social icons. Where Clinton used The White House to depict authority and power, Blair used sand-castle and British bulldog to connote authority, resilience and power. This is to be expected since the elections took place in two different parts of the world with different political systems and social set-ups. The setting of Bill Clinton's shots was reflective of his incumbency status while Blair approached it by using the less formal working candidate method.

The choice of icons and symbols were different. Whereas Clinton used icons such as the Oval office, the Capitol, the White House as background, Blair was on the streets interacting with the electorate by reaching out to them at work, at home and at play. He was seen playing tennis and soccer in two different scenes.

Rather than assume that one leader's political communication styles had been influenced by the other, perhaps it could be said that cross-national communication patterns were emerging. It is notable that in some of the allegorical use of language employed by Blair and Clinton, it would take more than mere knowledge of the English language to fully understand the underlying messages in them, even though one may be able to read the surface meanings.

However, with the contemporary global trend of ideological shift to the center, we may be experiencing a convergence of political issues across cultures such that politicians in Britain can travel to another country and be able to campaign effectively for votes.

The heavy reliance on the media of mass communication, which places great emphasis on sound-bites, visual effects and "telegenic" looks have compelled politicians to look and sound alike. Indeed, what may be occurring is the global manufacture of politicians by television and we are likely to find politicians that may appear to be clones of each other. But then, an analysis of this nature will soon find those types of politicians to be television-made clones rather than real clones of each other.

Could the similarities in the campaign styles be superficial? Yes. They appeared on the surface to be similar perhaps due to the similarities in the issues of focus, but the styles were evidently different. However, on the question of whether the British politician had copied American style campaigns, it could be answered yes, with a clause. This is because with the increasing use of television for campaign purposes, there has been an attendant convergence of production styles across cultures.

Since politicians have to adapt to the communication practices made possible by television, it is becoming increasingly popular to use similar styles of crowding words and images into spots and sound-bites. Negrine (1996) differentiates adaptation of political communication practices from adoption, and contends that similarities in media practices may be misconstrued as similarities in campaign styles.

Scammell (1998) identified indigenous factors that are present in campaign styles of politicians all over the world that are unique to them and their societies. Indigenous driving forces like "television and changing patterns of partisan identification", (p.254) are instrumental to the convergence of political communication styles which may be misconstrued as globalization.

The answer to the research question on a common feature identified in the two campaigns is that both leaders campaigned on similar agendas. They situated their parties right in the center of the ideological spectrum and broadened their appeal to attract middle class voters. In addition to this, they both campaigned on a "new label", positioning themselves as a better leader for the new party they led. This tied closely with the relatively similar philosophical language employed by both leaders. They approached issues from an optimistic and youthful perspective, not despondent or uncertain. This buoyed up the voters' confidence in their candidacy.

In all, therefore, it could be concluded that the similarities observed were largely superficial and never went beyond the surface. The youthful appearance of both candidates, pitched against older men, the shift in ideological orientations of the two political parties as well as the appeal to the same social group, the middle class and women, made it appear that they were using similar campaign styles.

However, if any similarities can be cited, it can be directly linked with the role played by television in politics across countries. The medium has thus become a very crucial part of the message. The fact that the medium of dispersing political communication is same in the two countries may be influential in assuming that political messages across the world is becoming convergent. Different political structures in countries may make this difficult, if not almost impossible.

To conclude that Tony Blair copied Bill Clinton in the last General elections in terms of political campaign styles is questionable. They campaigned on similar platforms so they may have sounded alike. It is true that they exhibited some common characteristics in their communication styles and there were obvious differences in the manner of delivery of the messages. Common features were noticed in the two campaigns as they relate to campaign themes and slogans, "new Labor" and "new Democrats". In addition to this, the messages were targeted toward similar social groups with similar concerns. Issues concerning welfare reform are as crucial in Britain, where incidence of single motherhood and teenage pregnancies is quite high level. They had their messages around other similar issues like tax cuts, support for education and healthcare reforms.

Production styles of the two campaigns were different. Whereas Bill Clinton's approach was direct with no underlying meanings in images and symbols, Tony Blair's was loaded with multi-level of meanings. The settings of Blair's commercials were more natural than those of Bill Clinton. Blair employed music with lyrics that tallied with the theme of his campaign, "things will get better."

There was a philosophical semblance in their messages. It could be said that issues of concern to both of them were reflective of deep thoughts about the future generation, better life for all and a general feeling of optimism. Britain can be better, said Blair while Clinton wanted Americans to join him to build a bridge to the 21st century. The closeness in their ages could be responsible for their similar optimism and hope that was reflected in their rhetoric.

There has been an increasing trend following the collapse of communism whereby industrialized countries of the world have shifted their ideological posture as it relates to their democratic institutions. No longer is it fashionable for countries to rigidly cling to extreme ideological spots. These changes have brought with them a shift in the way politicians address their issues and policies regarding political communication.

Leaders employ political discourses that reflect this global ideological shift so much that it may be misconstrued to be a convergence of political communication rhetoric. The situation between Bill Clinton and Tony Blair fell within this framework of ideological shift. If not examined very deeply, the misleading assumption that both leaders are clones of each other may be drawn.

The situation that surrounds both leaders is such that gives comparison industry a boost and an air of verisimilitude. Both attended Oxford, married lawyer wives, and belong to the baby boomer generation. They campaigned on similar ideologies with their appeal mostly directed toward the crucial middle class voters. As in most democracies across the world, both shifted their political parties away from the left to the center.

The research into the issue of Americanization of political campaign all over the world has attracted rich contribution from scholars. Swanson and Mancini (1996), Negrine (1996) and Scammell (1998) all agree that there are similarities in campaign styles across cultures. In the case of Britain, Kavanagh (1996) did remark that the influence from the United States on political campaigns is much more than the influence from across Europe.

Is it proper to assume that the importation of some campaign styles like the use of political consultants, emphasis on candidate image and higher television use for political communication are necessarily evidence that the rest of the world is copying America? Rather than assume that a unilateral movement of styles from America to other countries was the only case possible, there may indeed be a bilateral movement of influence. (Negrine, 1996). Butler and Ranney (1992) argue that it is the practice of politicians and the media, exploiting technical innovations and marketing approaches that have altered the appearance of elections. (p.4)

It was evident in this study that a convergence of political communication format rather than similarities of communication styles. The notion of seemingly identical campaign styles across countries is amplified by the global shift in political ideology. Many politicians seem to be saying similar things in their campaigns because global politics has changed since the melt down of the Iron Curtains.

The increasing role of television as a mass medium in political communication has further enhanced any such assumptions about campaign styles across cultures. Television formats are being copied and more and more politicians are mastering the art of addressing a mass audience, not the crowd that used to hail them during their whistle stops.

It is likely that despite the convergence of televisual styles across nations, significant differences in media systems may constitute a stumbling block in the emergence of uniform or standard global political communication styles. Adaptation will continue, as evidence showed in this study and adoption will only be possible where media systems are closely similar.

Between Tony Blair and Bill Clinton, there were certain similar surrounding circumstances in their two countries prior to the elections. Over their opponents, they possessed the winning appeal based on their youthful vigor. "Both rode to office on a wave of noted ennui after many years of conservative governments. Both capitalized on their youth and personal charisma. And both reshaped their parties" platforms with pro-growth, pro-business agendas." (*Time*, April, 28, 1997). Without forgetting their political traditions, they employed individual styles which enabled them interpret those traditions for a new age. (*New Statesman*, May, 1997).

A similar trend has been reported in other parts of Europe where it is fast becoming unfashionable to belong to the party of extreme ideological beliefs. There is a surge to the ideological center. It could be said, therefore, that as societies continue to respond to situations and re-align following the melting of the Iron curtains, they will borrow from one another in terms of political ideals and politicians may sound more alike in some ways.

Limitations and recommendations

This study was conducted to explore the depth of similarities in the campaign styles of two world leaders beyond mere superficial assumptions that had gained grounds in the media and political discourse. Two world leaders are not often compared except striking similarities, even if only on the surface level, have been identified. The elections that took place in the United States and Britain within six months of each other provided a good opportunity to explore the issue of similarities between Clinton and Blair more critically.

It would have been better perhaps, if such a comparison had been based on two election periods to allow for a wider database. Doing that would have meant that the timeliness of this study would not have negated the timeliness of this study because it would have meant waiting for Tony Blair to complete another term. A study of that scope may be conducted in the years ahead to see how much of Clinton's campaign styles Blair would have perfected.

The only snag, though, would be that the study may not present itself for examination at such an auspicious time as this one did. This study was done because of the closeness of the elections in Britain and the United States. It was possible, as the answers to the research questions posed indicated, that to establish whether Blair's campaign styles were similar to Clinton's did not require two national elections in both countries to gather enough database.

Perhaps a study of all the speeches of Blair and Clinton in their political career could form a good resource base for probing deeper into levels of similarities or differences. In the current study, the database consisted of the campaign video tapes of the two leaders gathered during just one national election in the two countries. The inclusion of an analysis of speeches may be a better tool for establishing whether they are similar or different in some other ways beyond what can be revealed in their campaign messages. This may focus on policy statements, international relations, economic, political and issues that they made pronouncements on. However, since this study only limits itself to the comparison of campaign styles, such an attempt would be looking beyond the purview of what this study purports to deliver. This may be a topic for some more ambitious research endeavor for the future.

Within the scope set by this study, that the research questions were adequately answered was indicative of being able to deliver what the research study set out to do at the beginning. In terms of the use of verbal codes, that is, attitudinal and metaphorical language, it was shown that they differed. Even though in their attitudinal use of language they expressed criticisms about their opponents, this is expected in the political arena. Metaphorical language use was not similar despite that both used metaphors to convey deeper meanings.

The shift in party ideologies of both the Democratic Party and the Labour Party accounted for the similarities in the dominant themes in the ideological analysis of the text. In that respect, it could be concluded that the ideological language was identical.

Communication acts were largely different. This is expected because of the close ties between language and culture. Although the themes explored were similar, the structure as well as the pitch used in the delivery were quite different. On the question about similarities in political discourse, it was found that the social categories that they addressed and the contexts were similar but story-telling styles were a bit dissimilar.

Both leaders applied different visual codes to get their messages across to their audiences. This was apparent in the manner Clinton employed incumbent strategy of drawing state insignia into the campaign visuals. Where Blair was seen in his living room, eating breakfast with his family, Clinton performed stately duties at The White House, using state symbols to convey authoritativeness. There were differences in the manner their individual experiences conveyed reality.

On the question of "Americanization" of British campaign styles, it has been widely acknowledged that the American campaign styles have had significant impact all over the world. Like the rest of the world the British fascination of the campaign styles used in America is a welcome expectation. In the past British leaders have been identified as looking towards America for some campaign input.

It was determined in this study that more than in any aspect of political campaign, the influence of Americanization on the British elections was more in the area of adopting typically American techniques. Political communication has changed in Britain over the past decade or so and even if the British will accept with some trepidation, the prominence given to Tony Blair the candidate was atypical of the British campaign strategy. The notion that the British politics is being coarsened by the American glamour and less party influence has become bothersome to politicians.

The Blair campaign team adopted the war room strategy as Clinton did in 1992 while the prospects of a first-time ever televised debate between contending leaders were aborted in the last minute in Britain. Major's campaign team dressed up an actor in chicken costumes to follow Blair around his campaign tours following Labour's last minute decision about participating in the debate. (Butler and Kavanaugh, 1997, p.88).

By and large, it was observed that the influence of the American campaign styles was apparent in the appropriation of some media and information management approach by the Labour campaign team. In Britain, Blair as party leader campaigned to have his party elected since this assured him of the Prime Minister's position, while Clinton campaigned to get himself elected. As a result Blair's replication of the Clinton war room strategy played a positive role in ensuring that party squabbles were not picked up by the media such that the party message becomes obscure. Labour effectively used this strategy even to the admiration of Clintonites who were sure the way Labour managed information, aided by modern technology would find "its way back to the next round of American elections." (Brown, 1997, p. 481.

In conclusion, therefore, associated factors like similarities in age, political ideology, and the yearning urge of the British media to discover their own version of a youthful leader with the Kennedy enigma may have prompted the comparison industry to make statements about how similar Clinton and Blair were. To the Americans, "the Clinton comparison is the only way to locate Mr. Blair in their experience, while the Brits yearn for the days when their leaders played as big a role on the world stage as America's." (*Economist*, May, 10, 1997 p.56).

The last German election stands out as an example of a situation where globalization of campaign styles may be said to have occurred. Schroeder was said to have looked toward Tony Blair in his campaign styles. He shed the Social Democratic Party's leftist image and dwelled on campaign issues that touched on middle-class sentiments. So it is logical to assume that there is a convergence of campaign issues across the globe such that camapign styles and rhetoric are becoming more and more alike.

However this may be true, one question is, which influenced which, shifting political ideologies or the global influence of television and campaign consultants? It is true that television changed the face of politics forever and has shifted politics away from being an issue-based contest to the center stage of visual images. Could this be held responsible for the similarities in campaign styles of politicians? Could it be that the dismantling of Communism has led to the death of political dogma whereby politicians are moving en-masse to the center of the ideological spectrum? This could be the case of chicken and egg.

Are there any reasons why Bill Clinton and Tony Blair have attracted so much attention based on their similar styles? There are leaders all over the world who share similar qualities with Clinton just as Blair but are never put side by side for comparison. For the Americans and the British, traditional relationship in the areas of international politics and global leadership has often fueled the need to search for twin copies of situations across the Atlantic. This will not be first time such has been done and certainly will not be the last.

Appendices

Appendix A

Text of Campaign Video Tapes of Bill Clinton

(i) **Future:** 30 seconds.

Today you will decide what she eats (baby swinging), you decide what she wears. On November 5th, you will decide what kind of America she will grow up in. Bob Dole and Newt Gingrich tried to cut vaccines for children, tried to slash college scholarships, let toxic polluters off the hook. President Clinton stopped them. Protecting education...Protecting clean water...her future. On election day, November 5, she is counting on you. President Clinton, building a bridge to the 21st century.

(ii) **Generic:** 30 seconds.

You work for your whole life in the hope for a secure retirement. That is why it is so wrong that Dole and Gingrich tried to slash Medicare $270 billion. Dole even voted to make it easier for corporations to raise pensions...Dole's risky tax scheme will balloon the deficit. Dole's risky tax scheme would threaten Medicare cuts again. Can we count on Bob Dole?

(iii) **Testimonial** on smoking policy: 30 seconds

Each day in America 3000 children take up smoking, 1000 will die from addiction.

Linda Crawford: My husband was a lobbyist for the tobacco industry. His final wish before he died of smoking related cancer was to convince children not to ever start smoking. President Clinton has the courage to take up the special interest. He banned

147

cigarette ads that target our children. When people attack the president's character, I think of my children and millions of others his leadership is protecting.

(iv) **Dole and Gingrich** attack. 30 seconds

Dole and Gingrich against a woman's right to choose, against family leave, against Brady Bill and assault weapons ban, cutting vaccines for children. Against higher minimum wage, cutting college scholarships.

Clinton and Gore: Brady Bill signed, higher minimum wage signed, college tuition tax deductible. $500 child tax credit. Internet access for schools, economic growth. 100,000 new jobs. When it comes to America's future, which drummer do you want to march to? Vote Clinton-Gore.

(v) **Rebuttal** 30 seconds:

Bob Dole desperate attacks. President Clinton signs lifetime ban on foreign lobbying by top officials. Dole and Gingrich took $2.4 million from foreign interest... A top Dole official fined $6 million for Hong Kong fund-raising scheme... An independent watch-dog says Dole is senator most responsible for blocking any serious campaign finance reform. Bob Dole, wrong in the past, wrong for our future, wrong for our future and wrong to turn to desperate attacks.

(vi) **Rebuttal 2** 30 seconds:

This Dole and Gingrich has all the facts wrong. President Clinton supports tax credit for families with children. For when Dole and Gingrich insisted on raising taxes on working families, huge cuts on Medicare, education, toxic clean up, Clinton vetoed it. The president's plan, preserve Medicare, deduct college tuition, save anti-drug programs but Dole and Gingrich said no to America's plans. The President's plan, meeting our challenges, protecting our values.

(vii) **Safety**. 30 seconds:

60,000 felons and fugitives tried to buy guns but they could not because President Clinton passed the Bill on November 30, 1993 while the five day wait background checks. But Dole and Gingrich vote No. 100,000 new police because President Clinton delivered on September 13, 1994 while Dole and Gingrich vote No. Strengthened school anti-drug program. President Clinton did it. Dole and Gingrich voted No again. Their old ways don't work. The new way. Meeting our challenges, protecting our values...

(viii) **Environment**; 30 seconds:

Head start, student loans, toxic clean-up, extra police force, anti-drug programs. Dole and Gingrich wanted them cut. Now they are safe protected in the 96 budget. Congress reach budget agreement because the president stood firm. Dole and Gingrich, deadlock, shutdowns, gridlock...President Clinton's plan, finish the job, balance the budget, cut taxes, protect Medicare, reform welfare, get it done, meet our challenges, protect our values...

(ix) **Stand with Clinton**; 30 seconds:

Head start, anti-drug programs for schools. 100,000 police to patrol our streets. Medicare, Medicaid. President Clinton stands firm. Balance the budget, cut taxes but protect our elderly, children and future. Stand with President Clinton as he tries to move America ahead.

(x) **Values**; 30 seconds:

America's values, student loans, extra police, anti-drug programs, America's values protected by president Clinton's budget agreement. Dole and Gingrich latest plan include tax hikes on working families. Up to 18 million kids face health care cuts, Medicare slashed 167 billion. Then Senator Dole resigns leaving gridlock Gingrich help created.

Clinton: Politics must wait, balance the budget, help reform welfare Meet our challenges, protect our values.

(xi) **Action**; 30 seconds:

Senator Dole told us he could do his job and run for president. That he was a doer not a talker. Then he told us he was quitting, giving up all the gridlock he helped create. Now all he offers are negative attacks. Meanwhile, the real work goes on, balancing the budget, reforming welfare, protecting Medicare, education and environment. Cracking down on violent crimes by a leader whose proven action speaks louder than words.

(xii) **Dole votes No**; 30 seconds:

The president bans assault weapons on September 13, 1994. Dole and Gingrich say No. The president passes family leave on February 5, 1993, Dole and Gingrich say No. The president stands firm- a balanced budget, protect Medicare, disabled children- Dole and Gingrich say No again. Now Dole resigns leaving the gridlock he and Gingrich help create.

President's plan – balanced budget, protect Medicare and reform welfare, do our duties to our parents.

(xiii) **Victims**; 30 seconds:

An officer killed in the line of duty.... A father gunned down at work, a student shot at school, a mother murdered in cold blood. Victims. Killed with deadly assault weapons. Bill Clinton did something no president has ever been able to accomplish. He passed and signed a tough law to ban deadly assault weapons. Bill

Clinton- Deadly assault weapons off our streets. 100,000 more police on the streets, expand the death penalty. That's how we protect America.

(xiv) **Dayton (Testimonial);** 30 seconds:

Lt. Randy Beane (Dayton Police Dept.)

"I started to walk up to a vehicle. That's when shots rang out. As quick as he could pull the trigger that's how quick the bullets were coming. I've never heard a weapon that loud and when I saw the officer go down, I knew there was no way I could get to him. He died later that night. President Clinton is right. Its not about politics, its about a ban on deadly assault weapons. Its about the new death penalty law. President Clinton is helping us make this a safer nation."

Text: President Clinton signed the law banning assault weapons. President Clinton expanded the death penalty to over 50 new crimes.

(xv) **George (Testimonial)** Sgt. George Rodriguez; 30 seconds:

"I was just terrified that was it. That was the last day of my life. Stopped in routine traffic on the freeway, approaching the vehicle, I noticed the driver very nervous. In a matter of three seconds he produced a semi-automatic weapon and shot at me five times. President Clinton is right. This is not about politics. This is about saving lives."

(xvi) **Protect**: 30 seconds.

Images of Medicare on a sick bed with fluctuating heart. Text runs and heart stops with time...

(xvii) **Morals:** 30 seconds

As Americans there are some things we do simply and solely because they are moral, right and good. Treating our elderly with dignity is one of these things. We created Medicare not because it is cheap or easy but because it's the right thing to do. Republicans are wrong to want to cut Medicare benefits and President Bill Clinton is right to want to protect Medicare, right to defend our decision as a nation to do what is moral, good and right by our elderly.

(xvii) **New York Emma**. 30 seconds.

Preserving Medicare for the next generation. The right choice but what's the right way? Republicans say double premiums, deductibles. No coverage if you are under 67, 270 billion in cuts but less than half the money reaches the Medicare trust fund. That's wrong. We can secure Medicare without these new costs on the elderly. That's the President's plan. Cut waste, control costs, save Medicare, balance the budget. The right choice for our families.

(xviii); **New York sand:** 30 seconds

There are beliefs and values that tie Americans together. In Washington values get lost in the tug of war but what's right matters. Work, not welfare is right. Tax cut for working families is right. These values are behind the president's balanced budget plans, values the Republicans ignore. Congress should join the president and back the values so instead of the tug of war, we come together and do what is right for our families.

(xix) **Wither**: 30 seconds

Finally we learn the truth how the Republicans want to eliminate Medicare. First Bob Dole: "I was there fighting the fight voting against Medicare- we knew it wouldn't work in 1965. Now Newt Gingrich on Medicare: "we don't get rid of it in round one, we don't think that's politically smart. We don't think that's the right way to go through a transition. But we believe its going to wither on the vine".

Voice Over: Republicans in Congress, they never believed in Medicare and now they want it to wither on the vine.

(xx) **Family:** 30 seconds.

Our families need Medicare, now we learn the truth. And now the Republicans in Congress want the president to cut a deal and let Medicare wither on the vine. No deal. The president will veto any bill that cut Medicare benefits, education or harms the environment. The president believes we must do our duty by our parents and provide our children with opportunity.

(xxi) **Threaten:** 30 seconds.

Voice Over: The truth on Medicare. Medicare, wither on the vine! But President Clinton will veto any bill that cuts Medicare benefits, education or the environment. Now republicans threaten to close the government down if the president wouldn't cut a Medicare and education. No deal. The president will do right by our elderly and our children.

(xxii) **Constitution**: 30 seconds: The constitution.

Presidents have used the power it gives them to protect our values. That's why the 42nd president is vetoing the Republican budget. The $270 billion Medicare cut violates our duty to our parents. Their $30 billion education cut destroys opportunities. Cutting environmental protection, increasing taxes on working people hurts us all. That's why President Clinton is vetoing the Republican budget. Standing up for what's right for "we the people".

(xxiii) **People:** 30 seconds:

Belle is doing fine but Medicare could be cut. Nicholas is going to college but his scholarship could be gone. Joshua is doing well but help for his disability could be cut. President Clinton: Standing firm to protect people. Matthew bought a house but will the water be safe to drink? Mike has a job but new tax in the Republican budget could set him back. President Clinton says, balance the budget but protect our families.

(xxiv) **Children:** 30 seconds.

America's children; seven million pushed toward poverty by higher taxes on working class. Four million children get sub-standard health care. Education cut $30 billion. Environmental protection, gone. That's the sad truth behind the Republican budget plan. The president's seven year balanced budget plan protects Medicare education and gives working families with children a tax break. It is our duty to America's children and the president's plan will meet it.

(xxv) **Slash** 30 seconds:

Images similar to previous commercial.

(xxvi) **Table** 30 seconds.

The Gingrich/Dole budget plan. Doctors charging more than Medicare allowed. Head- start, school anti-drug program slashed. Children denied adequate medical care. Toxic polluters let off the hook. President Clinton has put a balanced budget plan on the table. Protecting Medicare, Medicaid, education, the environment.

The president cuts taxes and protects our values but Dole and Gingrich just walked away. That's wrong – They must agree to balance the budget without hurting America's families.

(xxvii) **Infomercial**: 5 Mins.

When I ran for President four years ago, I said I will end welfare as we know it and make responsibility a way of life for those that have been on welfare. I wanted to make sure our children will look out their window each morning and see a whole community getting up and going to work. We are making good on that commitment. We've helped 43 states to experiment with their own welfare reforms. Today there is already 1.9 million fewer people on welfare than I took off with four years ago. And child support collections are up 50 percent almost $4 billion.

The welfare reform bill that I signed will help us finish the job with strict time limits on those on welfare and the toughest child support enforcement in history and guaranteed healthcare, childcare and nutrition for children. To give families the help they need as they move from welfare to work. Now we even have to work harder to see that the jobs and opportunities are there so that people can leave welfare and become permanent members of the work force. Our goal is to help the private sector create one million new jobs by the year 2000 for welfare recipients. Under our new law, states can take the money once used for welfare checks and use it to help business leaders to hire people off welfare. Hundreds have already agreed to meet that challenge and I want to make it easier for them and others to do it.

My plan will give businesses a tax credit for everybody hired off welfare and kept employed and give private placement firms a bonus for every welfare recipient they place on a job who stays in the job. By helping people receive paychecks not welfare checks. By reinforcing our most fundamental values of work family and responsibility we will break the cycle of dependency.

We will help families come together and stay together. We will build a strong, safer community. That is the way to build a bridge to the 21st Century. A bridge that will give every American a chance at better and brighter future not a bridge to the past. That choice is very important and that is why we urge every American to participate on election day. After all it is your vote that will decide whether we balance the budget that will protect Medicare and Medicaid, education and the environment.

It is your vote that will decide whether we give our children education that is key to opportunity and higher paying jobs. Whether we help every child to learn to read or log on to the vast world of the Internet and meet the highest standards of excellence. Whether every one that wants to go to college has the opportunity to go. Whether we even have a department of education to even stand up for America's children.

Your vote will decide whether we leave the lives of many Americans in dignity or dependence earning a pay check and not welfare check. Your vote will decide we make our families stronger with better and more affordable healthcare. The tools to succeed at home and at work. Children that grow up free from gang and guns, drugs and tobacco.

Your vote will decide whether we keep the Brady Bill and keep guns out of the hands of felons and fugitives, stalkers. Whether we keep the ban on deadly assault weapons and keep putting 100,000 police on our streets all across America. This is the last Presidential election of the 20th Century. But in anyway it is our first discussion on how we move forward into the 21st Century that is wide enough and strong enough for all of us to cross.

(xxix) **Bridge to the 21st century** (five minutes)

I want to build a bridge to the 21st Century where our families are stronger because they are safer and more secure. That is why we are working so hard this past four years to crack down on crime with comprehensive program, more police, tougher punishment and smarter prevention. We passed a tough crime bill which is putting a 100,000 policemen on our streets. Passed the Brady Bill which has already stopped 60,000 felons, fugitives and stalkers from buying guns.

Now we are extending that law to those that commit domestic violence from buying guns. We banned deadly assault weapons. Now we are working to ban cop killer bullets. We passed threes strikes and you are.. Are out to keep career criminals off the streets for the rest of their lives. We passed the violence against women crime bill and we already have 60,000 women that have called our hotelmen.

We are making our schools safer, drug free and gun free. We are using our anti-racketeering laws to target violent teen gangs and we are using the resources of the FBI to break up those gangs.

I appointed an American hero, four-star General... to be our drug Czar. This is a strategy to target our young people. We have expanded the drug penalty to drug kingpins, increased border patrol agents by 40 percent. Our approach is working.

We now have the lowest overall crime rate in a decade. There are more drug felons in prisons than ever before and regular drug use is down by 13 percent.

But we must do more. We all have a role to play. Demanding more responsibility from our young ones and teaching them right from wrong. We must finish putting those 100, 000 policemen on our streets. We must all work with our community police to fight crimes. We are taking driver's licenses away from those who drink and drive and while we know that 90 percent of our children are taking responsibility and staying away from drugs.

We have to find the other 10 percent before it is too late. That is why we are working with states to ask young people to take drug test before receiving a driver's license. Now my opponent has a different approach. He voted to stop a 100,000 new police, against the Brady Bill, voted to cut the safe and drug bill in half and even said he will repeal his assault weapons ban. That is no way to protect our families. My comprehensive anti-crime program will keep us on the right track. Keep crime going down...block by block, neighborhood by neighborhood, all across America.

Throughout this campaign we have tried to focus on ideals and not insults. We have done that because what really matters is the life and future of the American people and who can best lead us into the 21st Century. I have a philosophy I had tried to follow this past four years, create opportunity for all, reinforce responsibilities from all and help us to build a community where all Americans have a role to play.

Compared to four years ago, we are definitely on the right track. Ten and a half million new jobs, 60 percent cut in deficit, income rising for the first time in a decade, nearly two million people off welfare, the lowest crime rate in ten years. We are putting 100,000 new place on the streets and we have stopped 60,000 felons and fugitives from buying guns.

Our progress is only the beginning, now let us keep going and building our bridge to the 21st Century by focusing on what really matters in the lives of our people. What matters is how we strengthen our families. Strong families need first a strong economy that means balancing our budget to reduce interest rates on mortgages, car loans, from credit cards payments to car loans.

By doing it while protecting Medicare and Medicaid, education and the environment. This means giving tax cuts to families when they need it and mostly to raise and educate their families, to pay for medical emergencies, to buy that first home. It means working hard to make parents protect our children from gangs and guns, from drugs and tobacco. What really matters is how we finish the job of reforming welfare so that we can break the cycle of dependency for those families who are trapped in it.

We must move at least a million people from welfare to work and have got to do that in partnership with the private sector. What matters more than anything else now is how we give our children the best education in the world to prepare them for the 21st Century. We must make sure that every eight-year old can go on to college and ever worker can keep on learning for a lifetime. Now if we focus on these things on what really matters for our future, we will build that bridge to the 21st Century with more opportunity, more responsibility and a stronger community for all of us.

(xxx) DNC National Convention speech, Chicago. (100 minutes)

Thank you. Thank you. Come on. Sit down. We are going to start. Thank you very much. Thank you. Thank you. Thank you. Thank you very much. Thank you. (Applause continues)

Mr. Chairman, Mr. Vice President, my fellow Democrats, and my fellow Americans, thank you for your nomination. I don't know if I can find a fancy way to say this, but I accept.

So many, so many have contributed to the record we have made for the American people. But one above all, my partner, my friend, and the best Vice President in our history, Al Gore.

Tonight, tonight I thank the city of Chicago, its great Mayor and its wonderful people for this magnificent Convention. I love Chicago for many reasons. For your powerful spirit, your sports teams, your lively politics, but most of all, for the love and light of my life, Chicago's daughter, Hillary. I love you.

Four years ago, you and I set forth on a journey to bring our vision to our country, to keep the American dream alive for all who are willing to wok for it, to make our American communities stronger, to keep America, the world's strongest force for peace and freedom and prosperity, four years ago, with high unemployment, stagnant wags, crime, welfare, and the deficit on the rise, with a host of unmet challenges and a rising tide of cynicism, I told you about a place I was born, and I told you, and I still believed in a place called hope.

Well, for four years now, to realize our vision, we have pursued a simple but profound strategy, opportunity for all, responsibility from all, a strong united American community. Four days ago, as you were making your way here, I began a train ride to make my way to Chicago through America's heartland. I wanted to see faces. I wanted to hear the voices of the people for whom I have worked and fought these last four years. And did I ever see them.

I met an ingenious businesswoman who was once on welfare in West Virginia, a brave police officer shot and paralyzed, now a civic leader in Kentucky. An auto-worker in Ohio, once unemployed, now proud to be working in the oldest auto plant in America to help make America number one in auto production again for the first time in 20 years.

I met a grandmother fighting for her grandson's environment in Michigan. And I stood with two wonderful little children, proudly reading from their favorite book, the little engine that could. At every stop, large and exuberant crowds greeted me, and maybe more important, when we just rolled through little towns, there were children there waving their American flags, all of them believing in America and its future. I would not have missed that trip for all the world. For that trip showed me that hope is back in America.

We are on the right track to the 21st century. Look at the facts. Just look at the facts: 4.4 million American now living in a home of their own for the first time; hundreds of thousands of women have started their own businesses; more minorities own businesses than ever before; record numbers of new small businesses and exports.

Look at what's happened. We have the lowest combined rates of unemployment, inflation, and home mortgages in 28 years. Look at what happened. 10 million new jobs, over half of them high-wage jobs, 10 million workers getting the raise they deserve with the health insurance because the Kennedy-Kassebaum Bill says you can not lose your insurance anymore when you change jobs, even if somebody in your family has been sick. 40 million Americans with more pension security, a tax cut for 15 million of our hard pressed Americans and all small businesses. 12 million Americans, 12 million of them taking advantage of the Family and Medical Leave law so they can be good parents and good workers. Ten million students who saved money on their college loans.

We are making our democracy work. We have also passed political reform, the line item veto, the Motor Voter Bill, tougher legislation laws for Congress, stopping under-funded mandates to state and local government. We have got one more thing to do. Will you help me get campaign finance reform in the next four years?

We have increased our investments in research and technology. We have increased investments in breast cancer research dramatically. We are developing a supercomputer that will do more calculating in a second than a person with a hand-held calculator can do in 30,000 years.

More rapid development of drugs to deal with HIV and AIDS and moving them to the market quicker have almost doubled life expectancy in only four years, and we are looking at no limit in sight to that. We'll keep going until normal life is returned to people who deal with this.

Our country is still the strongest force for peace and freedom on earth. On issues that once before tore us apart, we have changed the old politics of Washington.

For too long, leaders in Washington asked, who's to blame? But we asked, what are we going to do? On crime, we are putting 1000,000 police on the streets. We made three strikes and you're out the law of the land, we stopped 60,000 fugitives, stalkers from getting handguns under the Brady Bill. We banned assault rifles, we supported tougher punishment and prevention programs to keep our children from drugs and gangs and violence.

Four years now, for four years now, the crime rate in America has gone down. On welfare, we worked with states to launch a quiet revolution. Today, there are 1.8 million fewer people on welfare than there were the day I took the oath of office. We are moving people from welfare to work. We have increased child support collections by 40 percent.

We are on the right track to the 21st century. We are on the right track, but our work is not finished. What should we do? First, let us consider how to proceed. Again, I say, the question is no longer who's to blame, but what to do. I believe that Bob Dole and Jack Kemp, and Ross Perot love our country. And they have worked hard to serve it. It is legitimate, even necessary to compare our record with theirs, our proposals for the future with theirs, and I expect them to make a vigorous effort to do same. But I will not attack, I will not attack them personally or permit others to do it in this party if I can prevent it.

My fellow American, this must be a campaign of ideas, not a campaign of insults. The American people deserve it.

Now, here's the main idea. I love and revere the rich and proud history of America. And I am determined to take our best traditions into the future. But with all respect, we do not need to build a bridge to the past. We need to build a bridge to the future, and that is what I commit to you to do. So tonight, tonight let us resolve to build that bridge to the 21st century, to meet our challenges, and protect our values. Let us build a bridge to help our parents raise their children, to help young people and adults to get the education and training they need, to make our streets safer, to help Americans succeed at home and at work, to break the cycle of poverty and dependence, to protect our environment for generations to come, and to maintain our world leadership for peace and freedom. Let us resolve to build that bridge.

Tonight, my fellow Americans, I ask all of our fellow citizens to join me and to join you in building that bridge to the 21st Century. Four years now, from now, just four years from now, think of it, we begin a new century, full of enormous possibilities. We have to give the American people the tools they need to make the most of their God-given potential. We must make the basic bargain of opportunity and responsibility available to all Americans, not just a few. That is the promise of the Democratic Party. That is the promise of America.

I want to build a bridge to the 21st Century, in which we expand opportunity through education. Where computers are as much a part of the classroom as blackboards. Where highly trained teachers demand peak performance from our students, where every 8-year-old can point to a book and say I can read it myself.

By the year 2000, the single most critical thing we can do is to give every single American who wants it the chance to go to college. We must make two years of college just as universal as four years of high school education is today, and we can do it. We can do it, and we should cut taxes to do it. I propose a $1500 a year tuition tax credit a year for Americans, a Hope scholarship for the first two years of college to make the typical community college education available to every American.

I believe every working family ought also to be able to deduct up to $10,000 in college tuition costs per year for education after that. I believe the families of this country ought to save money they spend on college. We'll get the money

Appendix B

Text of Tony Blair's Party Election Broadcast (PEB's)

(i) **Labor Business** (4mins 40 Secs.) City of London scene.

Proxy Narrator: Business is more powerful in government. It is quicker. It is more creative. Business is the lifeblood of the country. from this all the benefits the society needs, employment, investments, revenue for essential social programs. "I think frankly if there's any party that can represent Britain best, getting business right, and that party is New Labor.

(ii) **Testimonial by Anita Roddick, Founder, The Body Shop.** (4mins 40 secs)

"In 1976 there was just me, 21 years later we have over 1500 shops in 47 countries. One of the great myths of the 18 years is that the Tories are entrepreneurs. Entrepreneur is taking the situation that you have now and changing it. Now that isn't the thinking of the Conservatives. Mr. Major is a man surrounded by incompetence, the lack of strength, vision. It's palpable. I didn't vote Labor that last time, now they seem to be listening to the entrepreneurs and I think it will be an exciting time for British business. Whenever I spoke to Tony about his conviction I feel a sense of what Labor will give. I like the way he looks exhausted, I like the way he's working, and finally a politician that is not arrogant. Labor Party is definitely a party that business can do business with.

(iii) **Testimonial by Jonathan Charkham, Former advisor to the Bank of England**. (4 mins 40 secs.)

"I have been in business and worked as an advisor to the Bank of England. The government gets tired and it shows.

It's been showing terribly for the past two or three years. Why should it be perfectly natural for a businessman having looked at what the parties are doing and deciding to vote Labor? Gordon Brown is going to be a Chancellor. He will finally put to bed the idea that the Labor Party has to be a party of high taxation and spending. What they want to strive mightily to achieve is staging it in terms of inflation. It is only then will it be the confidence that is necessary for the log term investment which this country is crying out for.

(iv) **Testimonial by Terrence Conran, Design, Restaurant, Retailing:** (4 mins 40 secs)

"Habitat started in London in the early 60's and I tried to bring things well designed to the mass market. It got great reviews and gradually we expanded and became the catalyst for building something called storehouse. The turnover is about 1.5 billion Pounds a year. John Major is not strong enough to run a cabinet and keep that cabinet together. Now I do think that Tony Blair will be strong enough. I am impressed by his dynamism, his understanding of the importance of business to the economy and to the quality of life in this country."

(v) **Testimonial by Gerry Robinson, Chairman of the Grenada group.** (4mins 40 secs)

"I have been Chairman for Grenada Group for six months.... Granada is in a number of businesses. We have Grenada TV rental, catering and hotel interests, motorway operator, Little Chefs, Happy Eaters. We employ just under 80,000 people.

I think what I brought to the organization is clarity. I set out very clearly what I hope the organization can achieve and then lay out plans in order to achieve them.

Well, those skills are exactly the skills you need in running anything whether it's a business, party or country. See what Tony Blair has actually done in terms of creating new Labor. It is phenomenal change and I have no doubt at all in having set out very clear objectives for Labor in government. That Tony Blair will also deliver that, that's about leadership. That quality of leadership will come through again and again. Genuinely, one of the most refreshing things about this election is that the Labor Party is not saying that everything was wrong. I've always voted Conservative ever since I was old enough to vote. I have changed my mind and I am going to vote Labor on this occasion. For the simple reason that I believe is the right choice for Britain.

Text Reads: New Labor. Because Britain deserves better.

Lyric in background: "...Things will only get better..."

(vi) The Mill:(4 mins, 40 secs)

Proxy Narrator: As Britain approaches the end of the century, we have been with the same master now for 18 years. We still have the talent, skill and the inventiveness that we have always had. Probably more so in a rapidly changing world where we seem somehow to have lost our sense of purpose.(Bulldog is sleeping, snoring)

Now someone has emerged who is determined to give back to us. He is the most talked about politician in his generation. (Tony Blair seen with Nelson Mandela). They have called him everything from "Bambi" to "Union Basher", from "public opinion porter" to "Autocrat". One thing is undeniable in three short years his energy and leadership have transformed his party. What can he do for Britain?

Tony Blair: Look, the Tories didn't get everything wrong in the eighties, let us just be honest about that. Admit it, but Britain can be better. We can make this country better than it is. (Bulldog is still snoring).

The Tories today are no longer a party of low taxes. The fact is that they broke their word on taxes. They raised taxes 22 times. Ordinary families have had massive tax raises under the Conservatives. The largest tax in peace time history. Now I don't want to add to the burden of those families. They are hard working. I like to see them get that tax burden down. That's why we say we are not going to raise the basic or top rate of income taxes. (Bulldog becomes attentive but still sleepy)

Ask yourself this question. These Tories get back for another five years, we wouldn't even have a National health Service (NHS) in the way we've known and grown up with it. Now we have to rebuild the NHS and as a start we will spend 100 million Pounds by cutting that bureaucracy and putting it into cutting waiting list. Why should people in this country have to put up with these levels of crimes, the fear, the hassle, the abuse, elderly people often afraid to go out of their own homes, sometimes afraid to be in their own homes. The Labour Party will take on these issues in every single aspect of it. Tough on crime, tough on the causes of crime. (Bulldog begins to stretch as if shutting off sleep. It's still on leash though, owner holding onto it). I am a British patriot and I want the best out of Europe for Britain. We need a government that is going to lead in Europe not just follow along behind the Europe that is being shaped by others. A divided Conservative with weak leadership, fighting itself cannot fight for Britain. Education is the future for this country. If we don't give our children the right education they don't succeed and Britain doesn't succeed. That is why I have said for the Labor Party, its top three priorities, education, education, education. And again, we can make a start for example by reducing class sizes for all five, six and seven year olds in our primary schools to 30 or under. That we will do in the five years of Labor government. Britain can be better than it is and I'm not going to promise anything that I can't deliver. I do tell you that today's Labor Party transformed as it is with the strength of leadership and strength of unity behind it can make this country better'.

Voice over: After 18 years of weak leadership, incompetence and broken promises (Bulldog breaks away from leash). Britain deserves better. Give Tony Blair your mandate on May 1st and let him give Britain back its sense of purpose. New Labor, because Britain deserves better... (Lyrics: Things will only get better...)

(vii) **Digital locomotion facilities**. (4mins;40 secs)

Just imagine what would happen if the Tories got in again. Just imagine what the Tories would do with another five years. Under the Tories there are 50,000 fewer nurses. If the Tories get in again, they would continue to pull apart the NHS. The Tories would sell off homes for the elderly and abolish the state pension. Crime has doubled under the Tories. Then they promised 1,000 extra police. They actually cut 500. If the Tories got in again even more young criminals would go unpunished. Tory policies mean even more schools are now failing. If the Tories got in again it will even be harder to find a decent school. Last time, the Tories promised to cut taxes on heating. In fact, they introduced 22 new taxes since 1992. If they got in again they would put VAT on other essentials like food.

John Major's weak leadership would further reduce Britain's influence in the world. Just imagine what would happen if the Tories got in again. If they were give another five years. They'd do as they pleased and noting will stop them.

If the Tories were given another five years, they'd do as they pleased and no one would be safe and nothing could stop them. Britain deserves better. (Lyrics: Things will only get better)

(viii) **Labor Complete**. (4 mins 40 secs)

Tony Blair: "If you had said to me in 1976, I would have said forget it. Anything else but being a politician."

Q: Why, on what grounds?

Tony Blair: Because I felt politicians were complete big pain in the backside. You continually contemplate whether to stay in politics because of the complete rubbish you have to do and you just have to do it. You just have to get a grip of yourself and let your humanities see through and in the end understand why you want to be in it. What I keep saying to people is get behind the....It is really difficult for people to actually see the kind of person you are. My ambition when I was a young boy was to play football for Newcastle United and I kept talking my Dad into whatever media influence he had to get me a trial but he never did. Because my ad was very active in Tory politics actually locally and they even had him line up to be a member of the Parliament but then he became ill. So we gave up everything but we discussed it. Then when I started being Labor, the slight, but at that time he never really objected to it. Although he now came over to the Labor Party and says all is fine. I think my generation is trying a different type of politics which is rigid in strong values and conviction. (Blair is seen playing soccer)

It's not quite left and right like the way it's been before. I just think for a whole generation of people they thought if they are right and did well, then you became a Tory. People used to say if you bought a house or owned a home then you are a Tory which was a crazy stuff. I've always understood because that's why some people who have done well, who have come up in life and made it on their own felt the Tory Party was the party for them because it was the party of ambition and aspirations and the Labor Party wasn't.

I think that's why the Labour Party became too stuck in the past, too rooted and said that where you are and that's where you stay. I think today the position has changed around. What we have always wanted with today's Labor Party ids to be the party of aspirations... but say you are in a society with ambition but no lack of compassion.

Q: So, why aren't you a Tory?

Tony Blair: Because I think in the end people fulfill their ambition better in a society where people have some sense of duty towards other people.

Blair with his kids, doing homework; Blair: Homework. Yes, you have a lot of homework in the Labor party. you hate it. All the time you just go back to understanding why you are there and why you want to.

In a sense people have just got to understand that things can change. It's just so daft to think that things couldn't be better. I mean they could be better. Even if you just decided on the right education system. Education system and welfare are the only things you are worried about, then everything else stays the same. Ask me my three main priorities, education, education, education. The main job of a politician is to change the country in the way you think is right for the country. There is no point in being in it unless you want to change things. If all you want to do is sit in the office, by the desk, sign papers, then there is no point in doing it. It's like everything.. It's like what we did with the Labour Party. We had a clear series of objectives to modernize Labor Party, bring it up to date and do the same with the country and it can be done. So when I say education, education, education, what that means is not just pulling the specifics of policies, it means trying to put every single bit of drive and energy into changing the education system of this country. For me, education is just like trading your reforms, your laws for Margaret Thatcher To me education is a big passion, it should drive everything that we are doing. Which is why today it is so crazy that we spend more on employment than education.

Blair: if a family of people are living with no one working, how can the children grow up with any sense of the work ethic, any sense of turning up to work on time, earning of wage. And they start living in a different culture and a different society when that actually happens then all the other problems actually come with it. All the crimes, drugs and benefit bills...

When I talk of getting people off benefit to work it's not because I am uncaring. On the contrary, in honesty, the true way to get out of it is to say we are going to do something about it. The first step we are going to take to implement a program to take 250,000 young people off benefits and into work funded by one of the excess profit from the privatized monopolized private utilities.

They said the great new Labor Party is going to change the world. They are just cynical. People are just cynical about politics and politicians. For example for the few past years if a government has been promising the people something and has never delivered them. People have gotten to the point where they say you are all the same. What's the use nothing is ever going to make the difference. Of course the Tories in a sense delighted that because the people said we might as well stick with what we've got. You don't have to stick with what you've got. It is absurd to say Britain can't be better.

Old Lady: ... I was in the hospital, they had no pillows. They told me to bring pillows and blankets. They ran out of drugs and to take my blood pressure they couldn't get a machine that was working. The doctors and nurses are doing a hard job.

Blair: The reason that backlog in NHS is that we are spending a lot now on...What has really happened is that the Conservatives don't really understand why we've created the health services. The health service to me is a living, breathing symbol of what a decent civilized society should mean in practice. Helping people on the basis of their need not on the basis of their wealth.

Blair: When my father became ill when I was 10 or 11, he had a stroke and all our lives changed after that really. For the first 24 hours we weren't sure whether he was going to live at all. Then that was okay. When he came back home he just couldn't do anything he needed. It was very tough on him because he was a good public speaker. So all those things had to stop and he had to give up all his political ambitions and everything changed. The amazing thing was that he actually rebuilt his life and my mother nursed him for three years and taught him how to speak again. When my mother died when I was 21 you suddenly caught a sense of urgency to your life as a result of that. You suddenly think what a short time you've got. You better get on and get things done, you better do things.

(Lyrics. Things could only get better)

Blair: We must awaken and ignite in our people the hope that change can bring because the last weapon the Tories have, their final weapon is to spare its citizens. In telling the people it's the same package and telling them it really doesn't matter and it's all the same, nothing can ever change. Rubbish. Of course things can always change. They said well don't let Labor ruin us. I said to them Britain can be better than this. (song ends)

Blair: I couldn't imagine myself sitting in Downing Street, doing the job and having those things going on outside there and not just being in grief or some galvanizing force driving through the change to make things better. I couldn't imagine doing it. Britain deserves better.

(ix) **The Mill 2**(4 mins: 40 secs)

10:10 (Time shown); Rain falling Siren flashes to hospital. Polling Station closed. ER shown. Tory Bill board is shown. Father and daughter, walk out of Emergency Room hail a cab.

Father: Can you take us to...other side of the Park?

Driver: Number 26, isn't it Becky?

Becky: How did he know my name?

Driver: Terrible weather, terrible times. Did you vote this time Tom?

Father: I meant to but we've been in casualty all evening.

Becky: Dad, how does he know my name?

Driver: Of course you have. You hurt your arm didn't you? Must hurt though. Still things will get better. Shame the health system won't get better.

Father: You telling me, six hours we were in casualty.

Bibliography

Addato, Kiku, (1993). *Picture perfect: The art and artifice of public image making.* New York: Basic Books Publishers.

Akwule, R. (1992). *Global telecommunications: The technology, administration and policies.* Boston, MA: Focal Press.

Allen, G. (1997). "Let the grass grow." *New Statesman.* (Vol. 125 Issue 4315, p. 104).

"A fading British romance," (December 8, 1997). *The Nation.* p. 21.

Atkin, C. and Heald, G. (1976). "Effects of political advertising." *Public Opinion Quarterly*, (Vol. 40 Issue 2, Summer, pp. 216-228).

Axford, Barrie et al. (1992). "Image management stunts and dirty tricks: The marketing of political brands in television campaigns." *Media, Culture and Society*, (Vol. 14 Issue 4, pp. 637-651).

Barking, Steve M. (1984). "The making of a public in a political campaign. A participant observation study." *Political Communication and Persuasion*, (2, (3), pp. 251-262).

Bennett, W. L. (1977). "The ritualistic and pragmatic bases of political campaign discourse." *Quarterly Journal of Speech*, (Vol. 63:3, October, pp. 219-238).

Benson, T. and Barton, L. (1984). "Television as politics: The British view." *Quarterly Journal of Speech*, (Vol. 65 Issue 4, December, pp. 439-445).

Berg, V., Wenner, L., and B. Gronbeck. (1998). *Critical approaches to television.* New York: Houghton Mifflin.

Berger, A. A. (1997). *Narratives in popular culture, media and everyday life.* London: Sage Publications.

Bhatia, Vijay K., (1993). *Analyzing genre: Language use in professional settings.* London: Longman Group U.K.

Biocca, F. (Ed) (1991). *Television and political advertising: Signs, codes and images*, Vol. 2. New Jersey: Lawrence Erlbaum Associate Publishers.

Blair, T. (1996). "New world, New Left." *New Statesman*, (Vol. 125, Issue 4299, p. 5).

Blumler, J. G. and Thoveron, G. (1983). "Analyzing a unique election: Themes and concepts." G. Blumler (Ed.). *Communicating to voters: Television in the first European elections.* London: Sage. pp. 3-24.

Blumler, J. G., Dayan, D. and Wolton, D. (1990). "West European perspectives on political communication: Structures and dynamics." *European Journal of Communications*, 5, (2-3, June pp. 261-284).

Bourdieu, P. (1980). "The aristocracy of culture." *Media, Culture and Society*, (2, 3, pp. 225-254).

Brown, R. (1997). "American influences: The cult of spin." *Historical Journal of Film, Radio and Television*, (Vol. 17, Issue 4, October pp. 481-484).

"Building that bridge to a special relationship,"(December 8, 1997). *Time*, p. 19.

Buss, T. and Hofstetter, C. (1976). "An analysis of the logic of televised campaign advertisements: The 1972 presidential campaign." *Communication Research* (Vol. 3 Issue 4 October pp. 367-392).

Butler, D. and Kavanagh, D. (1997) *The British General Election of 1997.* London: Macmillan.

Butler, D., and Ranney, J. (Eds.). (1992). *Electioneering: A comparative study of continuity and change.* Oxford: Clarendon Press.

Chanslor, M. D. (1996). The effects of televised political advertisement on candidate image. *Dissertation Abstract International* (A-56/08, p. 2919).

Chillon, P and Schaffner, C. (1997). "Discourse and politics" in Van Dijk, T. A. (Ed.). *Discourse as social interaction.* London: Sage Publications. (pp. 206-230).

"Clinton-Blair chemistry may fuse US-British ties." (1997, May 1). *The Christian Science Monitor* (89; 109, p. 3).

"Clinton Clone." (1994, July 25). *US News & World Report.* (p. 25).

"Clinton, Dole campaign rated." (1996, September 1). *Campaigns and Elections,* (Vol. 17, Issue 9, p. 64).

"Clinton's slippery coat-tails," *Economist.* (1996, November 9). (Vol. 341, Issue 7991, p.68).

Cortazzi, M. (1993). *Narrative analysis.* Washington DC: The Falmer Press.

Devlin, L.P. (1997). Contrasts in presidential campaign commercials of 1996. *American Behavioral Scientist.* (40 (8) pp. 1058-1084).

Devlin, L.P. (1982) "Reagan and Carter's advertising me review the 1980 television campaigns." *Communication Quarterly,* (Vol. 30, Issue 1, Winter, pp. 3-12).

Diamond, E and Bates, S. (1984). *The Spot: The rise of political advertising on television.* London: The MIT Press.

Donohue, T.R. (1973). Viewer perceptions of color and black and white paid political advertisements. *Journalism Quarterly,* (Vol. 50, Issue 4, Winter, pp. 660-665).

Drescher, D. (1987). "A typology of international political communication: Factual statements, propaganda and noise." *Political Communication and Persuasion.* (4 (2) pp. 83-91).

"Echoes and soundbites," *Economist.* (1992, March 14). Vol. 322, Issue 7750, p.21.

Elder, C. and Cobb R., (1983). *The political uses of symbols.* NY: Longman.

Elliot, M. (1996, April 22). "Heard this talk before? Labor's Blair sounds eerily like Clinton 92." *Newsweek* (Vol. 27, Issue 17, p.51).

Faber, R. J. (1992). "Advances in political advertising research: A progression from If to When." *Journal of Current Issues and Research in Advertising,* (Vol. 14, Fall, Number 2. pp. 1-18).

Farrell, T. B. (1976). "Political communication: Its investigation and praxis." *Western Speech Communication* (40 (2), Spring, pp. 91-103).

Fairclough, N. (1995). *Critical discourse analysis: The critical study of language.* London: Longman Publishers.

Fiske, J. (1990). *Introduction to communication studies.* London: Routledge.

Fiske, J. (1987). *Television culture.* London: Metheun.

Foote, J.S. (1991). "Implications of presidential communication for electoral success." In Kaid, L. and Sanders, J. (1991). *Mediated politics in two cultures: Presidential campaigning in the United States.* NY: Praeger.

Foss, Sonja K. (1992). "Visual imagery as communication." *Text and Performance Quarterly* (Vol. 12, No. 1 Article 9, January).

Frith, K.T. (1997). *Undressing the ad: Reading culture in advertising.* NY: Peter Lang.

Frith, K. and Wesson, D. (1991) "A comparison of cultural values in British and American print ads: A study of magazines. *Journalism Quarterly,* (Vol. 68. Issue 1/2, Spring / Summer, pp. 216-223).

Galnoor, I. (1990). "Political communication and the study of politics." *Communication Yearbook,* 4, pp. 99-112.

Garramone, G.M. (1983). "Issues versus image orientation and effects of political advertising." *Communication Research* 10 (Jan), pp. 59-76.

Gerstle, J and Sanders, K. (Eds.). (1991). *Mediated political realities in two cultures: Presidential campaigning in the United States and France.* New York: Praeger, pp. 261-270.

Gerstle, J., Sanders, K. and Kaid, L. (1991). "Commonalties, differences and lessons learned from comparative communication research." In Kaid, L., Gerstle, J. and Sanders, K. (Eds.). (1991). *Mediated politics in two cultures: Presidential campaigning in the Unites States and France,* pp. 271-280.

Gramsci, A. (1971). *Prison notebooks.* New York: International Publishers.

Griffin, M and S. Kagan. (1996). "Picturing culture in political spots: 1992 campaigns in Israel and the United States." *Political Communication*, (13, pp. 43-61).

Gronbeck, B. E. (1992). "Negative narratives in 1988 presidential campaign ads." *Quarterly Journal of Speech*, (Vol. 78. No. 3 Aug., Article 4).

Grose, T. (May 5, 1997 "Lessons from the Yanks." *US News and World Report* (Vol. 122, Issue 17, p. 14).

Gross, L.S. (1995). *The international world of electronic media*. New York: McGraw-Hill.

Gudykunst, W and Kim, Y. Y. (1992). *Communicating with strangers: An approach to intercultural communication*. (2nd ed.). New York: McGraw Hill.

Guttenplan, D. (1997, December 8) "A fading British romance." *The Nation* p.23.

Gurevitch, M. and Blumler, J. G. (1990). "Comparative research: The extending frontier." In D.L. Swanson and Nimmo, D. (Eds.), *New directions in political communication*, pp. 305-325.

Gurevitch, M. et al. (1992). "Television spectacles as politics." *Communication Monographs* (Vol. 59, Issue 4, Dec., pp. 415-420).

Haiman, F.S. (1991). "A tale of two countries: Media and messages of the 1988 French and American presidential campaigns." In L. Kaid, Gerstle, J. and Sanders, K. (Eds.). (1991). *Mediated politics in two cultures: Presidential campaigning in the United States and France*, pp. 25-39.

"Heard this talk before? Labor's Blair sounds eerily like Clinton in '92." (1996, April 22). *Newsweek*, p. 56.

Hellweg, S. A. (1985). "Packaging the Presidency: A History and Criticism of Presidential Campaign Advertising" by Jamieson, and "The Spot: The Rise of Political Advertising on Television" by Diamond and Bates. *Journal of Broadcasting and Electronic Media* (29, 4, Fall, pp. 464-465).

"He's no Clinton clone," (1997, July) *The American Spectator*, p. 37.

Holtz-Bacha, C., Kaid, L. L. and Johnston, A. (1994). "Political advertising in western democracies. A comparison of campaign broadcasts in the United States, Germany and France." *Political Communication* (January-March 1994, 11, 1, pp. 67-80).

Howells, R. "The Labor Party." (1997). *Historical Journal of Film, Radio and Television*, (Vol. 17 Issue 4, October, p. 445).

Hughes, E. (1994). *The logical choice; How political commercials use logic to win votes*. Lanham, Maryland: University Press of America.

"Into the valley of death," (1996, April 20). *Economist* (Vol. 339, Issue 7962, p.50).

Jackson-Beck, M., and Kraus, S. (1980). "Political communication theory and research: An overview 1978-1979." *Communication Yearbook* (4, pp. 449-465).

Jamieson, K. H. and Campbell, K. K. (1997). *The interplay of influence:News, advertising, politics and the mass media*. New York: Wadsworth Publishing.

Jamieson, K. L. (1996). *Packaging the presidency: A history of criticism of political campaign advertising*. New York: Oxford University Press.

Jamieson, K. (1992). *Dirty politics: Deception, Distraction and Democracy*. New York: Oxford University Press.

Jasperson, A.E., and Fan, D. P. (2002). "An aggregate examination of the backlash effect in political advertising: The case of the 1996 U.S. Senate race in Minnesota." *Journal of Advertising* (31 (1) pp. 1-2).

Jhally, S. (1990). *The codes of advertising: Fetishism and the political economy of meaning in the consumer society*. NewYork: Routledge.

Johnson, K.S. and Elebash, C. (1986). "The contagion from the right: The Americanization of British political advertising." In Kaid et al (Eds.). *New perspectives on political advertising*. Carbondale: Southern Illinois University Press, pp. 293-313.

Johnston, A. (1991). "Politics broadcasts: An analysis of form, content, and style in presidential communication." In L. Kaid, Gerstle, J. and Sanders, K. (Eds.).

(1991). *Media politics in two cultures: Presidential campaigning in the United States and France.* New York: Praeger, pp. 59-72.

Joslyn, R.A. (1980). "The content of political spot ads" *Journalism Quarterly*, (Vol. 57, pp. 92-98).

Joslyn, R. A. (1984). *Mass media and elections.* New York: Newbury Awards Records Inc. (Random House).

Jowell, Roger et al. (1993). "The 1992 British elections: The failure of the polls." *Public Opinion Quarterly* (Vol. 57, Issue 2, Summer, pp. 238-263).

"Just like Bill? No, but like Clinton, Britain's Tony Blair has found success in the political center," (1997, April 28) *Time*, p. 12.

Kahn, K. F., and Kenney, P. J. (2000). "How negative campaigning enhances knowledge of Senate elections." In J.A.Thurber, Nelon, C.J. and Dulio, D.A. (Eds.), *Crowded airwaves: Campaign advertising in elections.* Washington DC: Brookings Institute, pp. 65-95..

Kaid, L. L. (2004). "Political advertising." In Kaid, L.L. (Ed.), *Handbook of political communication research.* Mahwah, N.J.: Lawrence Erlbaum Associates.

_____. (1997). "Effects of the television spots on the images of Dole and Clinton." *American Behavioral Scientist* (Vol. 40, (8) p. 1085).

Kaid, L. L., Gerstle, J. and Sanders, K. R. (1991). *Mediated politics in two cultures: Presidential campaigning in the United States.* New York: Praeger.

Kaid, L. L. and Sanders, K. R. (1978). "Political television commercials: An experimental study of type and length." *Communication Research* (Vol. 5 Issue 1, Jan., pp. 57-70).

Kaid, L. L., Nimmo, D. and Sanders, K. (Eds). (1986). *New perspectives on political advertising.* Carbondale: Southern Illinois University Press.

Kaid, L. L. and Davidson, K. K. (1986). "Elements of video-style: Candidate presentation through advertising." Kaid, L.et al (eds.) *New perspectives on political advertising.* Carbondale: Southern Illinois University Press, pp. 184-209.

Kaid, L. and Johnston, A. (1991). "Negative versus positive television advertising in US presidential campaigns, 1960-1988." *Journal of Communication* (No. 41 (3), Summer, pp. 53-64).

Kaid, L. L. and Holtz-Bacha, C. (Eds). (1995). *Political advertising in western democracies: Parties and candidates on television.* London: Sage Publications.

Kandiah, M. D. (1995). "Television enters British politics: The Conservatives Party's Central Office and Political broadcasting, 1945-55," *Historical Journal of Film Radio and Television,* (Vol. 15 Issue 2, June, pp. 265-285).

Katz, R. S. (1996). "United States of America." *European Journal of Research* (30: pp. 487- 492).

Kennedy, S. (1998). "New Labor and the re-organization of British politics," *Monthly Review* (Vol. 49 Issue 9, p.14).

Kepplinger, H. M. (1982). "Visual biases in television campaign coverage." *Communication Research* (Vol. 9, Issue 3, July, pp. 442-446).

Kepplinger, M. and Donsbach, W. (1987). "The influence of camera perspectives on the perception of a politician by supporters, opponents and neutral viewers." In Palez, D. L. (1987). *Political Communication Research: Approaches, studies, assessments.*

King, A., Denver, D., McLean, I., Norris, P., Sanders, D. and Sayd, P. (1997). *New Labor triumphs: Britain at the polls.* London: Chatham House.

Kenny, M. (1997). "Labor and life." *The Human Life Review* (Vol. 23, Issue 1, Winter, p. 53).

Knight, R. (1994, July 25) "Clinton clone?" *US News and World Report* (Vol. 117, Issue 4, p. 9).

Knight R. (1996, April 8). "The next Prime Minister of Britain? Labor's Tony Blair follows Bill Clinton's lead." *US News and World Report* (Vol. 120, Issue 14, p. 35).

Langrehr, F. and Caywood, C. (1995). "A semiotic approach to determining the sins and virtues portrayed in advertising." *Journal of Current Issues and Research in Advertising* (Vol 17, No1, Spring, pp. 32-47).

Larson, C. U. and Wiegele, T. C. (1979). "Political communication theory and research: An overview." *Communication Yearbook* (3, pp. 457-473).

Larson, C. (1982). "Media metaphors: Two models for rhetorically criticizing the political TV spot advertisement in Central States," *Speech Journal* (Vol. 33, No. 4, Winter, pp. 533-546).

Latimer, M. K. (1984). "Policy issues and personal images in political advertising in state election." *Journalism Quarterly* (61, 4, Winter, pp. 776-784, 852).

Latimer, M. (1985). "Political advertising for federal and state elections, images or substance?" *Journalism Quarterly* (Vol. 62, Issue 4, Winter, pp. 861-868).

Leeds-Hurwitz, W. (1993). *Semiotics and communication: Signs, Codes, Cultures.* Hillsdale, New Jersey: Lawrence Erlbaum Associates Publishers.

Lejune, A. (1996, December 23). "Danger! Election ahead." *National Review* (Vol. 48, Issue 24, p. 27).

Lemert, J. B., Wanta, W. and Lee, T. (1999). "Party identification and negative advertising in a U.S. Senate election," *Journal of Communication* (49, 123-134).

Lowry, R. (1996, May 6). "Staking out the center, *National Review* (Vol. 48, Issue 8, p. 21).

Lucaites, L. and C. Michelle Condit. (1988). "Reconstructing narrative theory: A functional perspective." *Journal of Communication* (Vol. 35, No. 4, pp. 90-108).

Maarek, P. (1995). *Political marketing and communication.* London: John Libbey.

Maicas, M. P. (1995). "The ethics of political communication." *European Journal of Communication* (Vol. 10 4 pp. 475-495).

"Major upset." (June 2, 1997). *American Spectator.* (Vol. 30 Issue 6, p. 86).

Mansfield, M. W. and Weaver, R. A. (1982). Political communication theory and research: An overview. *Communication Yearbook*, (5 pp. 605-625).

Marting, L. P. (1973). "British control of television advertising." *Journal of Broadcasting* (Vol. 17, Issue 2, Spring. pp. 159-172).

Marvin, C. (1994) "Fresh blood, public meat: Rituals of totem regeneration in the 1992 presidential race." *Communication Research* (Vol. 21, June, No. 6, pp. 264-292).

Mathes, R. and Semetko, H. A. (Eds.) (1991) "Foreword: A comparative perspective on television and election campaigns." *Political Communication and Persuasion*, (Vol. 8, No. 3, pp. 139-145).

Mazzoleni, G. (1991). "Emergence of the candidate and political marketing: Television and election campaigns in Italy in the 1980's," *Political Communication* (8, 3, July-September, pp. 201-212).

McAllister, I. (1985). "Campaign activities and electoral outcomes in Britain 1979 and 1983," *Public Opinion Quarterly* (Vol. 49, Issue 4, Winter, pp. 489-503).

McCombs, M. E. and Shaw, D. (1972). "The agenda-setting function of mass media," *Public Opinion Quarterly* (36, 176-187).

McHugo, G. (1985). "Emotional reactions to a political leader's expressive displays." *Journal of Personality and Social Psychology* (49, pp. 1513-1529).

McLeod, J. Kosicki, G. and Dianne, M. (1988). "Political communication research: An assessment of the field." *Mass Communication Review* (15, (1), pp. 8-15).

McNicholas, A. and D. Ward. (2004). "United Kingdom." In Lange, B-P. and Ward, D. (Eds.) *The media and election: A handbook and comparative study*. Mahwah, N.J.: New Jersey: Lawrence Erlbaum Associates.

Meadow, R. (1981). "The political dimensions of non-product advertising," *Journal of Communication* (Vol. 31 Issue 3, Summer, pp. 69-82).

Merrit, S. (1984). "Negative political advertising; Some empirical findings," *Journal of Advertising* (13, pp. 27-38).

Micklewait, J. and Wooldridge, A. (1996). "Managing to look attractive," *New Statesman* (Vol. 125, Issue 4309, p.24). Carbondale: Southern Illinois University Press, pp. 293-313.

Morreale, J. (1991). *A new beginning: A textual frame analysis of the political campaign film.* New York: State University of New York Press.

Morreale, J. (1991). "The political campaign film: Epideitic rhetoric in a documentary frame." In Frank Biocca (ed.). *Television and political advertising*, Vol.2; Signs, Codes and Images. Hillsdale: Lawrence Erlbaum. pp. 188-189.

Murray, N and Murray, S. B. (1996). "Music and lyrics in commercials: A cross-cultural comparison between commercials run in the Dominican Republic and in the United States." *Journal of Advertising* (Vol. XXV, No.2, pp. 51-63).

Negrine, R. (1996). *The communication of politics.* London: Sage

Nimmo, D. D. (1980). "Political communication: Information and image networks." *Communication* (5, (2), pp. 169-182).

Nimmo, D. and Combs, J. E. (1990). *Mediated political realities* (2nd ed.). New York: Longman.

O'Leary, S. and McFarland, M. (1989). "The political use of mythic discourse: Prophetic interpretation in Pat Robertson's Presidential campaign," Quarterly Journal of Speech (75, 4, November, pp. 433-452).

Patterson, T. E. (1991). "More style than substance: Television news in United States National Elections." *Political Communication and Persuasion*, (Vol. 8, pp. 145-161).

Patterson, T. E. (1980). *The mass media election: How Americans choose their President.* New York: Praeger Publishers.

Phillips, A. (1992, April 20). "John Major's surprise: British voters return the Tories for a record fourth straight term," *Maclean's* (Vol. 105, Issue 16, p.22).

Philo, G. (1993). "Political advertising, popular belief and the 1992 British general election," *Media, Culture and Society* (15, 3, July, pp. 407-418).

Porter, M. J. (1983). "Applying semiotics to the study of selected prime time television programs," *Journal of Broadcasting* (Vol. 27:1 Winter.

Potter, W.J. (1996). *An analysis of thinking and research about qualitative methods.* Mahwah, NJ: Lawrence Erlbaum.

Priest, S. P. (1996). *Doing media research: An introduction.* London: Sage Publications

Quere, Henri (1991). "French political advertising: A semiological analysis of campaign posters." In Kaid, L., Gerstle, J. and Sanders, K. (Eds.). *Mediated politics in two cultures: Presidential campaigning in the United States and France.* New York: Praeger. (pp. 85-98).

Reed, S. (1997, July 21). "Tony's secret weapon: Bill's experience," *Business Week,* (p. 48).

Riessman, C. K. (1993). *Narrative analysis.* Newbury, California: Sage Publications.

Roe, Keith. (1989). "Political communication research" by D. Paletz (ed.). *European Journal of Communication* (4, 1, March, pp. 122-123).

Roper, C. S. (1996). A cross-cultural analysis of the content of televised political advertisements in the United States and Italy. *Dissertation Abstract International* A-57/09.

Rosenbaum, M. (1997). *From soapbox to soundbite.* London: Macmillan.

Rosenberg, S. and McCafferty, P. (1987). "The image and vote: Manipulating voters' preference," *Public Opinion Quarterly* (51, pp. 31-47).

Roser, C. (1987). "New perspectives on political advertising," *Journal of Broadcasting and Electronic Media* (Vol. 31, Issue 1, Winter, pp. 105-107).

Rudd, Robert, (1986). "Issues as image in political campaign commercials," *Western Journal of Speech Communication* (50, 1, Winter, pp. 102-118).

Saint-Martin, Fernande, (1990). *Semiotics of visual language.* Bloomington: Indiana University Press.

Sanders, K. and Kaid, L. (1978). "The influence of speech communication on the images of a political candidate: "Limited effects' revisited," *Communication Yearbook* (1, pp. 465-474).

_____. (1978). "Political communication theory and research: An overview." *Communication Yearbook* (Vol. 2, pp. 375-389).

Scammell, M. (1998). "The wisdom of the war room: US campaigning and Americanization." *Media, Culture and Society* (Vol. 20, pp. 251-275).

_____. (1995). *Designer Politics*. Basingstoke: Macmillan.

Scammel, M. and Semetko, H. A. (1995). "Political advertising on television: The British experience." in Kaid, L. L. and Holtz-Bacha, C. (Eds.). *Political advertising in western democracies*. Thousand Oaks, CA: Sage.

Scott, J., and Zac, L. (1993). "Collective memories in Britain and the United States," *Public Opinion Quarterly* (Vol. 49, Issue 4, Winter, p.489-503).

Semetko, H. A. (1987). "Political communications: The general election campaign of 1983" by Ivor Crewe and Martin Harrop (eds.) and "Television coverage of the 1983 general election: Audiences, appreciation," *European Journal of communication* (Vol. 2, Issue 3, September, pp. 371-381).

_____. (1989). "Television news and the "third force" in British politics: A case study of election communication," *European Journal of Communication* (Vol. 4, Issue 44, December, pp. 453-479).

_____. (1991). "Parties, leaders and issues: Images of Britain's changing party system in television news coverage of the 1983 and 1987 General Election campaigns." *Political Communication and Persuasion* (Vol. 8, pp. 163-181).

Semetko, H., Blumler, J. G., Gurevitch, M. et al, (Eds.) (1991). *The formation of campaign agendas: A comparative analysis of party and media roles in recent American and British elections*. Hillsdale, NJ: Lawrence Erlbaum Associate Publishers.

Shyles, L. C. (1984). "Defining "images'of presidential candidates from televised political spot advertisements." *Political Behavior* (Vol. 6, No.2).

_____. (1983). "Defining the issues of a presidential election from televised political spot advertisements." *Journal of Broadcasting* (Vol. 27, No. 4. Fall).

Smith, A. (1991). *The age of behemoths: The globalization of mass media firms.* New York: Priority Press Publications.

Smith, L. D. (1991). "A narrative analysis of the American party platforms and the French Professions de Foi: Reality construction in two cultures." In Kaid, L., Gerstle, J. and Sanders, J. (Eds.). (1991). *Mediated political realities: Presidential campaigning in the United States and France.* New York: Praeger.

_____. "Convention oratory as institutional discourse: A narrative synthesis of the Democrats and Republicans of 1988," *Communication Studies* (1990) 41, No. 1, p.19.

Smith, L.D. and Nimmo, D. (1991). *Cordial concurrence: Orchestrating National Party Conventions in the telepolitical age.* New York: Praeger.

Speer, R. (1971). Myth, reality in the late eighteenth century British politics and other papers. *Quarterly Journal of Speech*, (Vol. 57, Issue 2, April, pp. 246-247).

"Staking out the center." (1996, May 6). *National Review.*

Stevenson, R. L. (1994). *Global communication in the twenty-first century.* New York: Longman.

Stiller, R. L. (1994). *Analyzing everyday texts: Discourse, rhetoric and social perspectives.* London: Sage Publications.

Swanson, D. and Mancini, P. (1996). *Politics, media, and modern democracy.* London: Praeger Publications.

Tak, J. (1997). "A cross-cultural comparative study on political advertising between America and Korea: A content analysis of presidential campaign ads from 1963 to 1992. *Dissertation Abstract International* A-654-11, p. 3919.

Tak J, Kaid, L, and Lee, S. (1997). A cross-cultural study of political advertising in the U.S. and Korea. *Communication Research*, (24:4, p. 413).

Tannen, D (Ed). (1993). *Framing in discourse*. New York: Oxford University Press.

"The American connection,"(November 8, 1997). *The Economist*.

"The visible hand," (September 20, 1997). *The Economist*.

Timmerman, David (1996). "1992 Presidential candidate films: The contrasting narratives of George Bush and Bill Clinton," *Presidential Studies Quarterly* (26: 2. pp. 364-373).

"Tony Blair and the new left: A new direction for Britain?" (March/ April 1997). *Foreign Affairs*

"Tony Blair New UK Prime Minister". (May, 1997). *Europe*.

Trent, Judith S. (1975). "A synthesis of methodologies used in studying political communication. *Central States Speech Journal* (26, 4, Winter, pp. 287-297).

Tucker, R., Weaver, R, and Benjamin-Fink, C. (1981). *Research in speech communication*. New Jersey: Prentice-Hall.

"Twin peaks," (May 10, 1997). *The Economist*. (342, 8021, p. 62).

van Dijk, T. A. (Ed). (1997). *Discourse as social interaction: Discourse studies, a multi-disciplinary introduction*. Vol. 2 London: Sage Publications.

_____. (Ed). (1985). *Handbook of discourse analysis*. Vol. 1. London: Academic Press.

_____. (Ed). (1997). *Discourse as structure and process: Discourse Studies, a multidisciplinary introduction*. London: Sage Publications.

Vogler, C. (1992). *The writer's journey: mythic structures for screen writers and storytellers*. Studio City, CA: M. Wiese Productions.

Waterman, R. W. (1996). "Storm clouds on the political horizon: George Bush at the dawn of the 1992 Presidential election," *Presidential Studies Quarterly* (26:2, pp. 337-349).

Webb, Paul (1996). "United Kingdom," *European Journal of Political Research* (No. 30, pp. 479-486).

West, D.M. (1993). *Air wars*. Washington, DC: Congressional Quarterly Inc.

West, Darrell, (1994). "Television advertising in election campaigns," *Political Science Quarterly* (Vol. 109, Issue 5, Winter 1994/1995, pp. 789-810).

Williamson, J. (1993). *Decoding advertisements: Ideology and meaning in advertising*. 9th edition. New York: Marion Boyars Publishers.

_____. (1984). *Decoding advertisements: Ideology and meaning in advertising*. New York: Marion Boyars Publishers.

Wilkinson, H. (1996). "Tony, the ladies' man," *New Statement and Society* (Vol 125, Issue 4310, p.26).

Wolton, D. (1990). "Political Communications: The construction of a model." *European Journal of Communication*. (5, March 1, pp. 9-28).

"Wooing Britain's middle class- "Clinton style'," (September 3, 1996). *The Christian Science Monitor*.

Worcester, R. M. and Harrop, M. (Eds). (1982). *Political communications: The General Election campaign of 1979*. London: George Allen and Unwin Publishers.

Zito, G. V. (1984). *Systems of discourse: Structures and semiotics in the social sciences*. London: Greenwood Press.

Zoonen, v. L., (1998). "A day at the zoo political communication, pigs and popular culture. *Media, Culture & Society*. (Vol. 20, pp. 183-200).

Index

STUDIES IN POLITICAL SCIENCE